MODERN FLY-CASTING METHODS

LEFTY KREH

THE LYONS PRESS
Guilford, Connecticut
An imprint of The Globe Pequot Press

The Lyons Press is an imprint of The Globe Pequot Press.

10 9 8 7 6 5 4 3 2

Printed in the United States of America

Color photographs by Lefty Kreh
Illustrated by Rod Walinchus

ISBN: 1-58574-789-0

The Library of Congress Cataloguing-in-Publication Data is available on file.

FRONTISPIECE: *Lefty teaching his modern casting method to a young lady at a Federation of Fly Fishing Conclave, Livingston, Montana.*

CONTENTS

INTRODUCTION

Of all the factors involved in fly fishing, none is so important as the ability to cast. And the better one can cast, the more likely the success in fly fishing, and certainly, the greater the pleasure. Of all types of casting — fly, plug, spin or bait — none is so much fun, in and of itself, as fly casting. You rarely see a spin or plug fisherman practicing his casting just for the fun of it. But you will frequently see fly fishermen on the lawn or at the water's edge, casting for long periods of time just for the fun of it. I liken such practicing to target shooting with a bow. The difference is that you don't have to bother walking to the target to retrieve your arrows, just make a back cast and start all over again.

People coming to the sport of fly fishing for the first time seem intuitively to recognize that casting is important. I have been teaching fly casting for more than 35 years. Whenever I question my students about what aspect of fly fishing they most want to learn, the majority always answer that more than anything else, they want to become good casters. It's a shame that only a relatively small percentage of anglers will eventually become first-rate fly casters.

Why is that? I think one of the major reasons is that even though many anglers may have initially learned good casting technique, they then failed to practice enough so that their technique could become ingrained and automatic, so they could consistently cast well when it really mattered, streamside where the fish are.

I've fly fished all over the world, and I can report to you that the most common complaint of guides everywhere is that so many of their clients come to the stream with surprisingly second-rate casting skills. I have never been able to account for this phenomenon.

People who take up the sport of golf, for example, will spend countless hours on the practice tee perfecting their swing. But without any fly casting practice whatsoever, these same individuals will, at great cost, purchase all the latest fly fishing equipment and tackle, and spend many additional thousands of dollars on travel, guides and lodging, only to reach streamside totally unprepared to cast well and fish successfully. They will return home angry and disappointed, frequently blaming their equipment, or their outfitter, or their guide, or the weather, for their failure to catch fish. And what's equally amazing, they will repeat this behavior year after year, over and over again!

Of course, there is another reason for poor casting — the lack of an understanding of what proper fly casting technique is. And no amount of practice will cure this deficiency, and in fact may even aggravate it.

I believe the material that I am going to present to you in this book — I call it my *modern method of fly casting* — will provide you with good technique. I think you will find that it is a method that is easy to learn, and that it will give you the necessary insights for you to master the essential casts that you will need for almost any fly fishing situation you may ever encounter.

But I cannot force you to practice. You've got to do that yourself. Whether you are a raw beginner or an experi-

Lefty casting to bonefish, Andros Island, Bahamas. ➤

enced fly caster seeking to improve your skill, I know you are sufficiently motivated or otherwise you would not have this book in your hands. So as we begin our little fly casting session together, I hope you'll make a promise to yourself — if you like my modern fly casting method and think it will work for you — to do your best to improve your fly casting technique with just as much determination as you bring to all the other meaningful activities in your life. That means practice. Practice. Practice! You'll make me happy, and make a lot of frustrated guides around the world happy, and of course, most importantly, you'll give yourself the lifetime gift of many hours of fly casting and fly fishing pleasure.

When I began teaching casting, instruction was based upon teaching the student to make a series of critically-timed mechanical motions, which when properly executed in sequence were supposed to result in the delivery of a good fly cast.

The standard method for teaching rod position and movement on the cast was the time-honored clock face method: begin the cast with the rod held out in front of you parallel to the water at nine o'clock, raise it quickly to a position directly overhead at twelve or one o'clock, then return the rod sharply to nine o'clock. Many instructors even insisted that you hold a book in the armpit of your casting arm during the cast, the idea being that if you dropped the book, you were moving the elbow and arm too much. Over the succeeding years, even though instructors eventually discarded the-book-under-the-arm idea, casting instruction essentially remained the same as it was taught in the early days.

Instruction in this clock face method was usually accompanied by the advice that timing was critical, and that one had to throw the line with a "power stroke." Then, once the basics of the clock face method, including timing and power stroke technique, were presented, the student was generally introduced to the mysteries of the double haul, a technique which, while it will increase line speed and increase distance on the cast, is extremely difficult for the inexperienced fly caster to master.

Using this method, with considerable frustration I struggled for years to teach my students to become good fly casters. But after several decades of first doubting and then questioning every phase of the traditional fly casting teaching method, I finally came to the conclusion that as far as I was concerned, it was more often than not a hindrance to the student learning to be a good caster.

You see, the problem with the traditional method — which even today is still being taught by most fly casting instructors — is that it is based upon the limited fishing environments, archaic techniques, and tackle that existed in Europe several hundred years ago when the sport began.

Let's look at how and where and to what species the first fly fishermen were casting their flies. While some of the earliest fly fishing was taking place in Spain and France, most of what we recognize as the beginning of fly fishing technique was being developed in Great Britain — usually by anglers who were presenting small flies to trout on chalk streams. These streams were quite small and narrow (a large one would have been little more than what we consider a long cast today). In fact, a few hundred years ago, *a long cast was perhaps 15 to 25 feet.* Today, unfortunately, because of modern industrial development and pollution, many of these historic streams now produce little or no trout and are consequently often ignored.

Since neither bamboo, fiber glass nor graphite was available in Great Britain at that time, early anglers had to use what was at hand for making their rods, which was wood.

Rods were made from a variety of native woods, principally greenheart. But often, combinations of two or three varieties of wood were used to achieve better rod action. A short rod was one of 11 to 12 feet in length. A long rod might be 14 to 16 feet in length; in fact, most rods were at least 14 feet long. Fly lines were usually made from several horsetail hairs braided into a single strand. Leaders were slices made from the gut of a cat. The total length of fly line and leader was perhaps six to eight feet long. Add 14 feet for the length of the rod, and the total length of the fly fishing outfit, from the rod handle to the fly, was more than 20 feet long — often longer than the width of the streams being fished! But since they were fishing only for trout on small streams, these pioneers found this type of tackle adequate for their purpose.

Probably quite naturally, I think, these early anglers developed a fine style of casting that was suited to the tackle and stream environments of their time. The rod was first lowered to about belt level of the angler (nine o'clock on the clock face), then swept upward to just beyond vertical (about one o'clock on the clock face), and then swept down and stopped.

For many years this method worked well, and so the nine-to-one-o'clock method became the standard for teaching fly casting. And because, like most great human institutions, fly fishing is built upon tradition, that same teaching method has been in use since the 1600s.

Now, tradition is wonderful, and remains one of the principal reasons why we enjoy the sport of fly fishing as we do. Yet, tradition frequently means doing things the way we used to do, which sometimes, I believe, is foolish.

When you consider that almost every aspect of fly fishing has changed since the 1600s (except the method used for teaching casting), you have to wonder why.

For example, look at the wet and dry flies used by those early anglers. In many instances they have no resemblance to the flies we use today. Take dry flies as an example. A visit to the American Museum of Fly Fishing in Manchester, Vermont — which I recommend that all fly fishermen visit — is enlightening in this regard. Many of the dry flies on display there, those used by anglers as recently as the turn of the century (including the celebrated angler Theodore Gordon and his contemporaries), are huge by comparison to today's dry fly patterns. These early American flies were tied on large hooks with big, soft hackles.

But in just the past few years, many of our top dry fly anglers have come to realize that the traditional "Catskill tie" of the dry fly (in which the fly stands off the water, supported on its stiff tail and hackle tips), is not as effective under difficult conditions as the no-hackle, paradun, thorax and parachute patterns.

The same degree of change exists in almost everything we do in fly fishing today compared to what anglers did in the 1600s, or even the 1900s.

You see, the art of fly fishing is a constantly changing game. One of the major attractions of the sport for many of us is that we can constantly experiment, try new concepts, and use different tackle and methods.

Yet we persist in teaching a method of fly casting developed centuries ago, despite the fact that every other aspect of fly fishing has changed. We no longer necessarily use small flies. We no longer use wooden rods. We have replaced the horsehair line with a vast array of specialized fly lines. In some cases, leaders (now made from space-age materials) can be nearly as long as the antique greenheart rod, horsehair line and leader combined!

Moreover, the method taught by almost all instructors today is based upon the idea that the angler will, almost always, be fly fishing for trout in small to medium-sized streams. For example, there is a highly advertised fly casting video that delves only into how to cast for trout while ignoring all other aspects of the sport.

Since trout fishing normally requires the throw of a short cast (usually less than 35 feet) and a fly dressed on a relatively small hook, the current method being taught can work, as is proven everyday by the thousands of trout fishermen who use it. But if you travel to where more difficult casts are frequently required, to our lakes and large rivers, or to the various fresh and saltwater fly fishing destinations around the world, you'll discover two immediate differences.

The first thing you will notice is that anytime the traditionally-taught angler has to make a difficult cast (throwing an extra-heavy fly, a long cast or a cast into a stiff breeze), if he is capable of doing it, he will employ the double haul technique. (We'll get into double hauling in more detail later in the book, but briefly stated, the double haul is a technique of pulling down on the line with the line hand in a certain manner on the back and forward casts to develop more line speed so the fly can be thrown farther.)

The principal reason the double haul was developed by the traditionalists was due to the inefficiency of the nine-to-one-o'clock casting method, so that some additional technique had to be invented to compensate for this deficiency. However, in the hands of the traditionally-trained angler, the double haul becomes a *crutch* to support a weak technique, not an efficient *tool* — as it is in my modern system of fly casting — for developing greater line speed in extraordinary casting situations, as I will be explaining later.

Another thing you will observe is that almost anyone who has mastered throwing a long line, has confronted a constant wind, or has developed a way of throwing bulky wind-resistant flies, will not be using the traditional method — especially if he or she was not taught by a traditional casting instructor. Instinctively, these anglers have from experience learned that the nine-to-one-o'clock method simply doesn't work, and have, almost unconsciously I suppose, developed a different technique that lets them cast with considerably less effort.

After teaching fly casting professionally for more than 35 years, I now believe that most of the fly casting instruction given today with use of the traditional method is difficult for the student to understand, much less utilize successfully; and that the method actually hinders the student from becoming a really good fly caster, regardless of the good intentions of the instructor.

So, I no longer teach the old method of going through a sequence of rigidly controlled and precisely timed movements to make the cast. Rather, I have developed five basic principles or rules which give the student a thorough understanding of what fly casting is, as well as what is a proper and improper technique. No sequence of rigid movements is taught — rather motions are made with the rod hand to accommodate the five principles. Also, with a good understanding of the five principles, a student should be able to observe and critique his or her own casting. And he will learn that a good cast is not a mystical movement, but is rather based upon common sense and simple physics.

Also, while in the nine-to-one-o'clock method anglers are encouraged to use their wrist for delivering the final portion of the cast, I feel, instead, that use of the forearm *with little or no wrist* not only delivers a more efficient cast, but also accommodates women, older people, children, and others who do not possess adequate power or strength in their wrist. Too many times I have seen anglers who use the nine-to-one-o'clock method for small stream trout fishing try to cast a heavy salmon rod, handle a tarpon rod, or make a longer cast on a steelhead river, only to fail because they didn't possess sufficient wrist strength. By using the method I have developed, these same anglers would be able to cast efficiently and with much less effort.

Another significant difference between the current method being taught and the method that I advocate is that with my method, timing is far less critical. With a cast of 40 or 50 feet, using the nine-to-one-o'clock method, the angler must come forward at the precise instant that the rod is loaded. But with the method I advocate, there can be as much as a three-second difference in the cast. The resulting cast is a good and efficient one. This ability to make casts within a longer time span allows a greater margin of error.

Yet another advantage of my method, I think, is that with a clear understanding of these five principles, a student should be able to observe and critique his or her own casting. Because if you want to become a good fly caster, you must know, on those occasions when you do something wrong, what you are doing wrong, and when in the cast you are doing it!

Since the method I teach is vastly different from the old standard method of teaching fly casting, if you have learned your technique with that method, I urge you, as you are introducing yourself to my five principles, to try to put out of your mind the rigid clock face method of learning rod positions that has almost always been used to teach fly casting technique in the traditional way. Try to avoid, for example, asking the question I am frequently confronted with in my classes — "Where do you do this motion or that movement?" — from students who have been led to believe that they can become good casters by memorizing specific rod positions on a clock face. *Forget about the clock face as a device to learn casting!*

Now, I have nothing against clocks. They're hard to beat for telling time. And since all of us are familiar with the clock face, the numbers on the clock are a convenient tool for fly fishermen to communicate with each other — for boat guides to point the angler in a proper casting direction for a sighted fish, for example. Or I will sometimes use the numbers on the clock face when I want to identify a particular direction. But I do not employ the clock face as it is used in teaching the traditional method, that is, as a mechanical or artificial device for learning casting technique by moving and stopping the rod in a rigid and precise sequence of fixed positions on the clock.

Instead, if you will begin your examination of my five principles with an open mind, and really study and think about them, I think you will discover and understand when and where to do something during the cast quite naturally, without using a clock face or any external teaching device, and that you will be able to make successful back or forward casts very easily at any time from any rod position.

I believe you will also discover that my five principles can be applied to all types of fly casting, from throwing a tiny midge dry fly to a sipping trout on a chalk stream to casting a huge streamer fly to a seven-foot sailfish.

And I honestly believe that by learning and understanding these principles, you will gain lasting insight into what fly casting is really all about.

Following the discussion of casting technique, I will then turn to a more detailed explanation of the essential casts that I believe you need to master in order to become a really first-rate fly caster.

OVERLEAF: *Mack Kantarian casting to trout on the Conowaga Creek, south-central Pennsylvania.*

CHAPTER ONE

THE FIVE PRINCIPLES OF LEFTY KREH'S MODERN FLY CASTING METHOD

PRINCIPLE NUMBER ONE

The rod is a flexible lever which moves through varying arc lengths depending upon the casting distance required.

ILLUSTRATION 1 — This principle applies to all casting circumstances, whether it's a simple upstream trout cast, or a roll cast, or a cast into the wind, or a long distance cast. The more you need help on a cast, the longer you want to move the rod through an arc on the back cast, and the longer you want to move the rod through an arc on the forward cast.

. The fly rod is really nothing more than a flexible lever, as any physicist will tell you. So the more difficult the cast, in other words, the more wind you have to throw into, the heavier the fly you have to throw, the farther you have to throw the fly . . . any time that the cast becomes more difficult, you should move the rod through a longer arc so that the momentum that is created by the rod motion through the longer arc will help the efficiency of the cast.

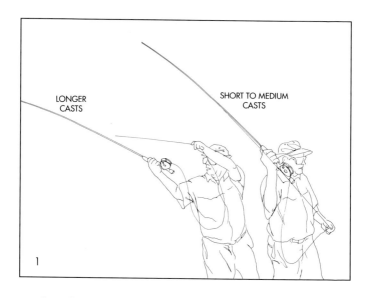

LONGER CASTS

SHORT TO MEDIUM CASTS

1

That does not mean that you move the rod through a longer arc for all casts. You simply move it though different arc lengths depending upon how difficult the cast is or how much rod power you need. For example, if you're going to throw a cast that's only 20, 25, or 30 feet, then you only have to take the rod up to the vertical (or twelve o'clock) position.

If you're going to throw a cast at 50 feet on a calm day, you may want to bring the rod up to the one or two o'clock position. If you're going to throw a 90-foot cast or have to throw into the wind or in other difficult situations, you may want to bring the rod almost parallel to the ground behind you, to a position of approximately three o'clock.

Additionally, by making the rod travel through a longer arc on both back and forward casts, the resulting tip movement will help you get rid of unwanted slack, as all slack must be removed from the line before casting. This motion will also allow you to lift a longer line from the water or throw a heavy, wind-resistant fly into a breeze with much less effort.

With the traditional method of moving the rod tip from belt level to a little past vertical (nine to one o'clock) for all casts, including long or difficult casts, the rod is doing little to assist the caster. For that reason, more effort has to be expended by the angler using this method, and often, as I have mentioned earlier, he will have to employ the double haul as a crutch to achieve greater distance.

In this regard, the traditional method seems even more ridiculous when you compare fly fishing to other sports in which we need to propel an object farther. When we make any kind of throwing motion in an attempt to propel an object farther or with greater speed, we naturally and unconsciously move the arm farther back. For example, in golf, when swinging the club to hit the ball a long distance, the golfer brings the club far back and makes a long sweep. In baseball, a pitcher winds up and takes his arm through the longest possible arc before throwing a fast ball. In tennis, when a player wants to smash the ball or needs a hot serve, he similarly brings his arm and racket through a very long arc.

You can test this theory yourself with a stone. You'll notice that if you want to throw a stone a short distance, the position of your hand as you start the throw will be near your ear. But if you want to throw a stone as far as you can, you will instinctively take your arm back far behind you — really as far back as you possibly can.

So, again, when you consider that it is natural to move the arm through a longer motion when a longer and/or faster throw is desired, it remains a mystery to me why modern instructors persist in teaching the traditional fly casting method of moving the rod through short arcs.

Here is a final point that I think you should keep in

mind. It is generally agreed among professional fly casting instructors that the major fault of most fly casters is that they begin their cast by holding the rod tip too high above the water, frequently shoulder high or even above the head. But since the rod tip is going to travel through an arc as the back cast is made, the higher you start with the rod tip, the more likely you will throw the line down behind you. But the lower you position the tip before the back cast is made, the better your chances for throwing the line at an upward angle behind you.

On most casts, particularly on longer casts, the rod tip should be below the belt before you start to make the back cast. The longer the cast, the lower the rod. On a very long pick-up, when you are picking up 60, 70, 80 or 90 feet of line, I believe you should actually touch the rod tip to the water to get the maximum amount of help from the rod.

If fly fishermen would begin all casts, except the very short ones, by lowering their rod tip near or even onto the water's surface, they would improve their casting skills dramatically. This idea needs repeating, I think: *almost all casts of any difficulty or length should start with the rod tip positioned below the belt.*

PRINCIPLE NUMBER TWO

You cannot make a cast until you get the end of the line moving; and on the back cast, the end of the line should be lifted from the surface of the water before the cast is made.

ILLUSTRATION 2 — This principle deals with one of the major faults of many fly fishermen: they try to begin their back cast before they get the end of the line moving. But the principle does not mean that you can make a cast when the

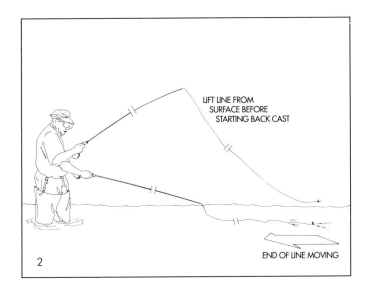

LIFT LINE FROM
SURFACE BEFORE
STARTING BACK CAST

END OF LINE MOVING

2

end of the line is moving, because the line could be drifting on the current, or be placed in motion by the wind. *You*, not the water's current or the wind, have to get the end of the fly line moving yourself.

As an example, consider that you are going to pick up one end of a long rope lying on a dock. If there is a good deal of slack in the rope, when you pull on one end, the other end doesn't move. But, with the rope in your hand, if you back away from the dock until all the slack is removed and the rope has become straight, and then jerk upon it, the entire rope will move.

It is just the same with a fly line. You cannot begin to move the fly on either the back or forward cast until you have gotten the end of the fly line moving. It is only then that you can make your cast.

Another potential problem exists before the start of the first back cast, when the line is lying on the water's surface in front of you. That is, surface tension grips the line and will not easily allow its release. People often don't take into account the power of this surface tension. And of course, the more line that is lying on the water, the stronger the grip of the surface tension on that greater amount of line.

The effect of this surface tension on the fly line may be better understood by considering two examples.

You may recall from your high school science class the experiment of placing a needle on the surface of water in a cup. Despite being heavier than water, the steel needle surprisingly remained floating on the surface of the water, demonstrating that surface tension acts like a barrier in water — even supporting a needle's weight.

Or, you can test this theory on your own with a fly line that has been designed to be heavier than water. With someone to help you, take a length of fast-sinking line (such as a *Scientific Anglers' Hi-D* line) and carefully lay it, stretched out lengthwise, on the water's surface of a swimming pool. When both of you gently release the ends of the line, you will find that despite its well-advertised capacity to sink rapidly, the line floats! Of course, it is being supported in this static situation by surface tension.

On your first back cast, there are three reasons why you want to get all of the line off the surface of the water before making the cast:

1. You will be able to make the back cast with much less effort, especially if you are picking up a long line.
2. If you start to propel the line behind you while a portion remains on the surface, your rod will bend with the effort. As a result, when the remaining line tears free from the grip of the surface tension, a jolt on the rod will be created, which in turn will cause the rod tip to undulate, forming shock waves in the line that will prevent making a good, smooth back cast.

3. The line may rip violently from the surface, creating a sudden disturbance and leaving a trail of minute foam and bubbles which will frighten wary fish.

On the forward cast, the same principle applies in reverse. You must get the end of the line moving. But since on the forward cast the line should be in the air behind you, all you need to do — assuming there's no slack in the line — is to bring your rod forward in order to get the end of the line moving.

PRINCIPLE NUMBER THREE

The line and the fly are going to go in the direction in which you accelerate and stop the rod tip at the end of the cast.

ILLUSTRATION 3 — As you study this principle, don't lead yourself to think that I am talking about the accelerations

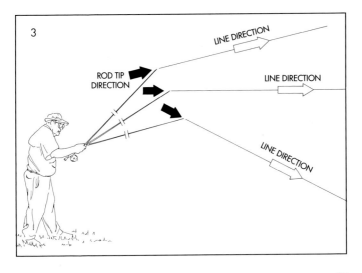

and stops that you make with your hand, even though your hand and rod are both going in the same direction. The line is going to go in the direction in which you accelerate and stop not your hand, but your *rod tip*. This is an important point, frequently overlooked by many fly casters, which creates all kinds of casting difficulties for them.

For example, if on your forward cast you accelerate and stop the rod the way many anglers do, with the tip coming down even below their chin level, your tip is going to go towards the water on the stop, creating two major problems: first, you will have created a big sag in your line which detracts from the effectiveness of the balance of your cast; and second, you will cause your fly line and leader to crash down on the surface of the water in front of you.

Or to provide another example, if you want to make a curve cast, you cannot make an acceleration and stop going straight ahead and then attempt to sweep the rod around the desired curve. If you do, as many anglers do when attempting this cast, then the fly is going to go straight ahead. If you want to make a curve cast, *you must accelerate at the end of the cast with the rod tip going in the direction you want the curve to be, and you must stop the rod tip in the direction where you want the fly to land at the end of the cast.*

This principle applies to both back and forward casts, as there is no basic difference between a back and forward cast. The same physical principles account for a good back cast and a good forward cast.

So regardless of what you do during the early stages of either the back or forward cast, the line and fly will always attempt to go in the direction in which you accelerate, or speed-up-and-stop, the rod tip at the very end of the cast.

Don Hathaway casting to sockeye salmon on an Alaskan river. ➤

The size of the fly line loop is determined only by the distance that you accelerate the rod tip at the end of the cast. And the faster that you accelerate over that distance, combined with a quick stop, the farther the cast will travel.

ILLUSTRATION 4 — This fourth principle involves *loop size* and *line speed*, the two factors that create distance in the cast.

Let's first look at how you build or make a loop during the cast, along with the relationship that exists between the caster's effort and loop size — perhaps one of the most misunderstood concepts in fly fishing.

When you make a back cast, the line from the tip of the rod to the fly is straight. You only create a loop after you have stopped the rod. Then a loop forms at the end of the line as it unrolls behind you. In the same way, when you

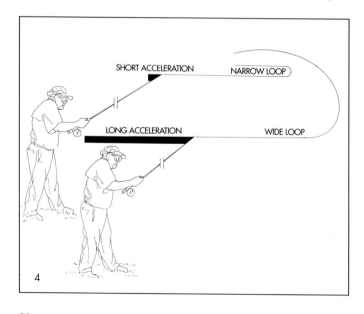

SHORT ACCELERATION   NARROW LOOP

LONG ACCELERATION   WIDE LOOP

4

make your forward cast, you have initially created a straight line, and the loop forms only after you have stopped the rod at the end of the cast.

Now, many people are under the illusion, because it has been written so often, that the principal reason that big loops don't go anywhere is that they are air resistant. But air resistance has little to do with this phenomenon. The reason that big loops don't go very far is that the caster's energy is being thrown around a half circle. The larger the loop, the more the line is unrolling around a large curve — some of the caster's energy is being directed overhead, some toward the target, and some down toward the water.

The smaller you make the loop size, however, the more your energy will be directed towards the target. Thus when you are able to make smaller loops, you will need less effort to make longer casts.

The principal reason why a small loop travels farther than a large loop is that you are actually aiming the energy of your cast in the direction you want it to go. So most of the time — not always — you want to throw a small loop, because it makes for more efficient back and forward casts.

The question then is: how do we make small loops? The size of the loop is determined by only one factor — nothing else: *the distance that you accelerate the rod tip at the end of the back and forward casts.* I do not mean the total distance that the rod moves backwards or forwards on the cast; but the distance the rod tip travels during the very quick speed-up-and-stop, or accelerated motion, that you make right at the *end* of each cast. *The shorter the distance that you move the rod tip rapidly at the end of the cast, combined with a quick stop, the smaller or tighter the loop.*

When poor casters get into trouble, near the end of their casts they start sweeping the rod tip through greater arcs. But this movement only dissipates their energy over an even wider area. Keep in mind what actually forms the loop. *When you accelerate the rod tip at the end of the cast, the tip never travels in a perfectly straight line, but in an arc. The shorter the distance of acceleration, the smaller the arc.*

So, if the tip accelerates at the end of the cast through an arc of six inches, then a cast with a six-inch loop will occur. But if the tip accelerates at the end of the cast through an arc of three feet, then a three-foot loop is formed.

If you clearly understand the idea that the accelerated distance of the arc at the end of the cast is what creates loop size, then you'll understand that the shorter the tip travels during that distance, the tighter the loop.

There is another important consideration involved with mastering this casting principle. You cannot achieve great distance or propel an air-resistant fly to the target by simply throwing a tight loop. A tight loop helps, but it is *line speed* that determines how far a line will travel. *The faster that a rod tip is moved over that brief distance, and the quicker you stop it, the faster the line speed and the farther the line will go.*

You can test this theory with a simple experiment. Sweep the rod forward as you would in a normal cast. Near the end of the cast, accelerate the rod tip slowly over a short distance. You will create a small loop as a result. But you'll see that because you didn't sweep forward swiftly and stopped rather slowly, the cast didn't go very far, even though the loop was small.

Now, repeat the exercise, making the rod tip travel through the exact same accelerated distance or arc. This time, however, move the rod tip much faster and bring the rod tip to a quicker stop. You'll see that the same size loop forms, but now it travels considerably farther.

So when making a longer or more difficult cast, you have to move the rod tip through its arc at a greater speed, and stop the forward motion of the rod tip more quickly.

I want to emphasize further that it is the speed of acceleration, not the strength of the caster that helps move the rod tip over the short distance. *A properly executed cast is made with a speed stroke, not a power stroke!*

Once you've learned the dynamics of these movements, you'll also gain a better understanding of why it is a mistake to use the wrist to make a cast. For most people, use of the wrist on the cast results in the formation of a wider loop and a drain of wasted energy.

Expert fly fishermen have the ability to move the wrist an incredibly short distance in order to prevent moving the rod tip a long distance during acceleration. However, it's a technique that takes years to learn and master.

For quicker and more accurate results, I suggest instead that you use your forearm during the end of the cast. But never use the whole arm, just the forearm.

For your own clarification of this technique, try this on a cast. Make a slow backward motion with the rod, as if you were initiating a back cast. Then, using only the forearm (don't bend that wrist!), make a brief acceleration stroke or a speed-up-and-stop motion at the end of the cast. Note how short a distance the tip travels during the acceleration at the end of the cast if the motion is made only with the forearm instead of the wrist. Repeat this exercise several times, using the forearm, so you can clearly determine just how far the rod tip is traveling at the end.

Now, make several more casts using the same motion, only this time, do it the wrong way by bending the wrist while accelerating the rod. You will see that this motion causes the rod tip to travel considerably farther at the end of the cast, creating a much larger loop, and in effect, throwing energy around a circle.

The average caster will have more success, I believe, if he uses only the forearm to move the rod through the casting arc. He will be able to accelerate the rod tip over a shorter distance, stop more quickly, and deliver a much tighter loop.

If you insist on bending the wrist, bear in mind that it generally takes people years to perfect this stroke, since it is difficult to train the wrist to move a short distance. But if you do insist on using the wrist, be aware that the longer the distance the rod tip moves, the greater the loop size.

Finally, also be aware that *a small amount of hand motion will be greatly magnified at the tip of the rod.* You can easily test this by holding a nine-foot rod horizontally in front of you. While looking at the front of the rod handle, rock the rod back and forth so that the front end of the handle moves sideways over a two-inch arc. You'll observe that the rod tip is simultaneously moving as much as eight to ten feet! So if you bend your wrist during casting, you'll be forcing the rod tip to travel over a surprisingly long distance, thereby creating large, inefficient loops.

To those of you who are already good casters, I warn you in advance that this fourth principle will be the most difficult aspect of my casting method for you to adapt to and master. This is because many experienced casters have a difficult time in accepting the fact that the shorter and faster the acceleration, the longer the cast.

For years they have been trying to execute their long distance casts by making long and powerful sweeps of the rod on their back and forward casts, which as we've discussed, generally just serves to produce large loops and reduced distance.

And I'll also caution those of you who run into this problem that your difficulty will probably not happen on your back cast, where as an experienced caster you probably, almost unconsciously, make a single haul on the line; because that single hauling motion, in and of itself, generally serves to improve the timing of your acceleration on the back cast.

The problem will more commonly occur on your forward cast, where most of the time you will not have used a hauling action, and will therefore not have had the assistance of a haul in timing your rod acceleration.

If you are encountering loop size and/or casting distance problems, keep in mind this critically important principle of good casting technique that *if you shorten your rod tip acceleration distance, you will increase your casting distance.*

PRINCIPLE NUMBER FIVE

For long or more difficult casts, you will need to bring the rod well behind your body on the back cast. In order to do this, you should rotate your casting thumb away from its normal position on top of the rod about 45 degrees away from your body before initiating the back cast, and then take your forearm (never the wrist) straight back 180 degrees from the target.

ILLUSTRATION 5 — It is not necessary to move the rod through a long arc for an easy or short cast; therefore when making a short cast the rod hand has only to be moved a short distance, no further than about even with the shoulder. If a somewhat longer cast is required, then the hand should be brought back perhaps a little beyond the shoulder.

For executing a very long cast, however, the rod hand will have to be extended back beyond the shoulder so that upon completion of the back cast, your arm will be extended nearly straight behind you. This motion requires a special technique that I want to discuss with you.

Normally in fly casting, the rod is held with the thumb on top of the handle. For short casts, when the rod hand and forearm are brought up and accelerated to make the back cast, the thumb remains on top of the rod handle

5

throughout the cast. But when executing a longer cast with the thumb in its normal position, it becomes impossible, because of the way we're built, to take your forearm behind you: it hits and stops against the bicep.

In order to compensate for this restriction of movement, some casters dip the thumb downward over the shoulder at the end of the cast, which causes the rod tip to travel farther back and downward. This technique also causes the rod tip to travel over a longer arc during the acceleration period, thereby creating two problems for the caster. First, keeping in mind that the size of the loop is determined by the distance the rod tip accelerates (Principle Number Four), when you bend the wrist down and back over the shoulder, the rod tip tends to cover too much distance and forms a big, inefficient loop. And second, keeping in mind that the line is also going to go in the direction in which the rod tip stops (Principle Number Three), the line is going to go down behind the caster, resulting in a deep sag.

Others try to hold onto the normal thumb position on the top of the rod handle, but rotate their hand outward. This movement does allow the angler to move his hand well back, but creates the same problems that were created by dipping the thumb downward. If the thumb is turned outward and moved backward, the line will unroll outward on the back cast and travel in a wide, open loop so that the angler's energy is being thrown around a wide curve, rather than correctly traveling straight back away from the target.

Others make an acceleration, and then "drift" the rod tip, so that the rod can be taken back farther on the back cast. Many casting instructors advocate this "power stroke and drift" method, but if the movement is not made correctly — which frequently happens with novices — the rod, as it is lowered, will drag the loop open and place sag in the back cast. This "drifting of the rod" technique requires a great deal of practice before it can be done with precision, and I do not recommend its use except by the most experienced fly casters.

The best way to overcome the restricted movement of your forearm is as follows. Hold your rod in the standard position with the thumb on top and with your thumbnail in full view. Then rotate your hand outward from the body at about a 45-degree angle — whether you're right or left-handed, it works the same way — just rotate the hand out. That means that the bottom of your hand, rod, and reel, will all come slightly in towards you at a 45-degree angle. When you have done this, you will now be getting a side view of about half or three-quarters of your thumbnail.

Now, you will find that with a motion similar to thumb-ing a ride, or hitch-hiking, with your thumb leading the way — and without breaking the wrist — you can sweep your forearm straight back and extend it completely behind you. You are really making a modified side cast.

Because of your hand rotation 45 degrees outward before the initiation of the cast, your back cast will really be describing an oval. As you make the hitch-hiking motion the rod will be sweeping back sideways to your body; but as you complete the back cast and are almost simultaneously making ready for the forward cast, as you direct the rod straight at the target in front of you, you will naturally be bringing it into a vertical position just as you initiate your forward cast.

A good way to check that you are doing this right is to look behind you at your rod hand upon completion of the back cast. Your thumbnail should be hidden from view. If you can see it, you did not execute a proper back cast, either because you broke your wrist, giving you a sag in the line; or you rotated the heel of your hand in the wrong direction, not towards but away from your body, which resulted in a wide looping back cast.

As your forward cast comes forward, by the time your forearm has traveled back to its normal casting position opposite your shoulder, your rod hand should be even with, or slightly in front of, your face. And as you complete your forward cast, you will see that your hand has come back to its normal starting position, with the thumbnail in full view on top of the rod.

Since the most efficient back cast is one that travels 180 degrees from the target, or exactly on a line straight away from it, it is particularly critical in using this technique for the long distance cast that *you make the cast only with the forearm*, not with the entire arm or the wrist. And since all back casts should normally rise at least a little (or else they may be directed into the water), while the forearm is traveling 180 degrees directly away from the target, it should also be moving upward at whatever angle of flight that you have chosen for your cast.

CONCLUSION

As you study these five principles, you'll see that any cast (the back cast or the forward cast, as they are simply identical motions in different directions) is really composed of only two sectors or areas of motion.

During the first sector of the cast, with the rod lowered, you must first get the end of the line moving, then gradually accelerate the rod through an arc of varying lengths, depending upon the length of cast you wish to make.

During the second sector of the cast, you should accelerate the rod tip over a short distance and bring it to a quick stop. Four important factors occur during this acceleration-and-stop sector, which when understood, will help in improving your casting and overall technique:

From Principle Number Three ...

1. *The direction in which you move the rod tip and stop it will determine the direction of flight of the line and the fly.*

And from Principle Number Four ...

2. *The distance the rod tip moves during the speed-up-and-stop period at the end of the cast will determine the loop size of the fly line.*
3. *The faster that the rod tip is accelerated at the end of the cast, the faster and farther the line and fly will travel during the cast.*
4. *The quicker that the rod tip stops at the end of the cast, the faster and farther the line and fly will travel during the cast.*

OVERLEAF: *Angler casting on a trout stream in North Carolina's Great Smoky Mountains.*

CHAPTER TWO

LEFTY KREH'S MODERN FLY CASTING METHOD

In order to show you how these five casting principles combine to create what I call my modern method of fly casting, I'm going to demonstrate the longer or more difficult cast, where in addition to my first four principles (which apply to all types of casts, short and easy, or long and difficult), I will be able to include my fifth principle, which only applies to the long or more difficult cast.

Therefore, as you study these illustrations, you will see all five of the principles at work:

1. *Your rod is a flexible lever which moves through varying arc lengths depending upon the casting distance required.*
2. *You cannot make a cast until you get the end of the line moving; and on the back cast, the end of the line should be lifted from the surface of the water before the cast is made.*
3. *The line and fly are going to go in the direction in which you accelerate and stop the rod tip at the end of the cast.*
4. *The size of the fly line loop is determined only by the distance that you accelerate the rod tip at the end of the cast. And the faster that you accelerate over that distance, combined with a quick stop, the farther the cast will travel.*

5. *For long and more difficult casts, you will need to bring the rod well behind your body on the back cast. In order to do this, you should rotate your casting thumb away from its normal position on top of the rod about 45 degrees away from your body before initiating the back cast, and then take your forearm (never the wrist) straight back 180 degrees from the target.*

SIDE VIEW

6

ILLUSTRATION 6 — Begin with the rod tip nearly at the water's surface. Remove all slack. For this long cast, the thumb of the rod hand should be rotated outward (away from the body) about 45 degrees. Important: *Don't use the entire arm to make the cast. Don't use the wrist. The cast should be made only with the forearm.*

ILLUSTRATION 7 — Use the thumbnail as an indicator of direction of travel of your rod hand. At the beginning of the cast you should be able to see your thumbnail. Then lift the rod smoothly and rather quickly. It is important that you

7

don't lift it slowly. If you do, the line immediately outside the rod tip will sag and create slack. But if you lift the rod too quickly, you will cause the line to come free from the surface of the water too vigorously, creating a sudden disturbance and leaving a trail of minute foam and bubbles which will frighten wary fish.

Illustration 8— For good casting it is necessary to make a back cast that travels directly away (or at 180 degrees) from the target. And since you don't want to throw your fly and line in the water behind you, all of your back casts should rise at some degree of elevation. Remember, never make the acceleration period at the end of the back cast until all line has been lifted from the water.

Since the line is going in the direction in which you accelerate the rod tip at the end of the cast, the rod hand and forearm must travel straight back and at an upward angle. And during acceleration, *the rod hand and forearm should move swiftly over a very short distance upward and directly away from the target. If at the very end of the cast you*

8

make your acceleration period exceedingly swift and make your stop very abrupt, you will make a very good cast.

As you complete this motion, the line will be traveling rapidly in a very tight loop directly away from the target. It is also important to understand that you should not accelerate the rod tip and then "drift." The rod should be brought back almost to the point where the cast will end, and only then should the acceleration be made. Note in the illustration that on a very long cast the rod arm has been fully extended behind the caster. Important: *the farther you want to reach behind you, the lower the angle you should move backward with the rod hand. With an extended (straight-arm) reach behind you, the back cast becomes almost a side cast.*

ILLUSTRATION 9 — At the end of the back cast, if performed properly, the thumbnail cannot be seen by the angler. An unseen thumbnail is an indication that the rod hand was brought straight back from the target. With a correct cast, the angler also should be able to look back and see the rod and fly line traveling in a straight line that will result in the creation of a tight loop.

9

If a wide loop was formed on the back cast, the acceleration period was too long, or the wrist was bent during the acceleration period, or the entire arm — rather than just the forearm — was held straight as it moved back. Using the entire arm to make the back cast will cause the line to travel in a wide arc and create an open loop behind the caster.

ILLUSTRATION 10 — For this long cast, the angler has rotated the thumb of his rod hand about 45 degrees outward so that his forearm will avoid hitting his shoulder, and this has

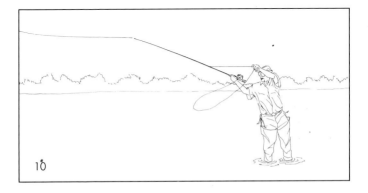

10

caused the rod hand and forearm to travel at a side angle on the back cast. As the forward cast is initiated, the hand is brought in close to the body. The entire movement — from back cast to forward cast — travels in an oval path.

11

ILLUSTRATION 11 — By the time the angler's shoulders have reached the position shown in the illustration, the rod should be coming forward in a vertical plane with the thumb directly behind the handle.

ILLUSTRATION 12 — Once the rod has reached a vertical position to the side or in front of the angler's head, the acceleration period can be made at any time the caster desires, provided all the line is moving (remember Principle Number Two). This illustration shows, for a normal cast, where the forward acceleration (or speed-up-and-stop motion) is being made to direct the line and fly at the target. The acceleration of the rod hand should be directed as straight ahead toward the target as possible. Don't use the wrist to

12

make the acceleration, or you will cause your rod tip to travel in a much wider arc, throwing line around a curve and wasting energy. Make the acceleration movement only with the forearm.

Most of the time the angler will want to direct the cast at eye level, not down at the water. Note the high position of the rod as forward acceleration stops. The majority of anglers end their forward stroke in a downward motion. This results in tearing the loop apart and causing much of the energy of the cast to be directed toward the surface, rather than at the target.

ILLUSTRATION 13 — At the end of the cast the acceleration stroke must be directed at the target. Principle Number Three says that the direction in which you accelerate and stop is where the line and fly will travel. But if during acceleration you direct the rod tip directly at the target and do nothing else, you will create a serious casting error, the tailing loop. I will discuss tailing loops later in the book. For right now, accept the fact that as soon as the abrupt

13

stop occurs after the acceleration, *you must dip the rod tip ever so slightly to avoid a tailing loop.* But if you dip the rod tip too far, you will open your loop and detract from the distance you can cast. Only dip the rod tip enough so that you are aware you have moved the thumb downward toward the surface — no more.

FRONT VIEW

ILLUSTRATION 14 — From a front view, you'll note that the rod tip has been lowered until the tip is near or touching the surface. If you are right-handed, you should have the left foot positioned forward. The reverse is called for a left-hander. This will allow for a smooth body flow as you reach back on the back cast. Some casters position both feet evenly, which restricts the body's natural movements. When making an extra-long cast, I will pick up the rear foot and step back with it as the rod arm travels way back behind

14

me. This helps me move the rod through a longer arc and allows my body to flow back and forth naturally.

ILLUSTRATION 15 — On this long distance back cast, the rod hand is traveling at a 45-degree angle, or side angle, on an oval path directly back and away from the target. The arrow points to the direction of acceleration and stop of the rod tip — which should be 180 degrees away from the target.

15

ILLUSTRATION 16 — The entire cast is performed in an oval. The rod sweeps back on the back cast at a side angle, but as the angler is getting ready to make the forward cast, as illustrated here, the rod is brought to a vertical plane before the cast is made.

ILLUSTRATION 17 — The final moments of the forward cast are made with a brief acceleration directly ahead and toward the target. As soon as the acceleration and stop are made, the rod tip is dipped downward just a little bit to avoid a tailing loop.

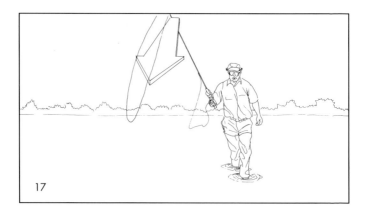

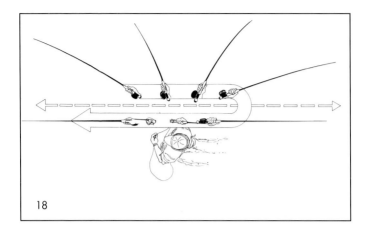

18

ILLUSTRATION 18 — This illustration is intended to demonstrate how for a long or difficult cast the rod travels well out
to the side on the back cast, but then upon conclusion of
the back cast, it is brought around in an oval path to bring
it into a position to prepare the angler for his forward cast
directly at the target.

OVERLEAF: *Lefty casting to trout on the Gunpowder River,
central Maryland.*

CHAPTER THREE

MASTERING
THE
ESSENTIAL CASTS

LOOP SIZE AS A DETERMINANT OF
LINE SPEED AND DISTANCE

ILLUSTRATION 19 — Principle Number Four states that the size of the loop is completely controlled by the distance that the rod tip is accelerated at the end of the cast.

A cast is composed of two sectors. The first is that period from the start of the cast just before the acceleration is made (you might say the period when one is preparing for the cast). The second sector of the cast is the acceleration of the rod tip and the stop.

This illustration shows what happens to most casters. They throw a fairly large loop, generally either by making too long an acceleration, or by breaking their wrist, or both. A large loop causes the caster's energy to direct the flight of the line around an arc, rather than directly at the target. And since the arc causes the rod tip to end in a downward direction, a portion of the energy of the cast is being thrown

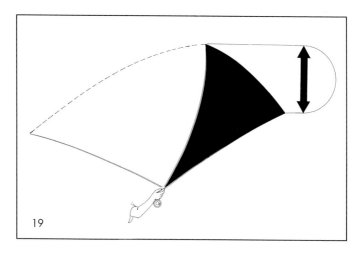

not at the target, but downward in front of the caster. Thus with a wide loop, energy is being thrown around a curve and much of it is wasted in the wrong direction.

ILLUSTRATION 20 — This illustration shows that the rod tip has been moved forward until everything is ready for the last portion of the cast — the acceleration and stop. During acceleration, it is almost impossible for the angler to move the rod tip in a perfectly straight line; instead, it travels in an arc. If the acceleration period is exceptionally short, and the stop is extraordinarily abrupt, the rod will travel through a very short arc, forming a tight loop. The abrupt stop also creates additional line speed, so that the line and fly will travel a longer distance.

Perhaps the most important considerations involved in good fly casting technique are embodied in the acceleration and stop sector. Let me emphasize three:

1. *The shorter the acceleration, the tighter and more efficient the fly line loop size.*

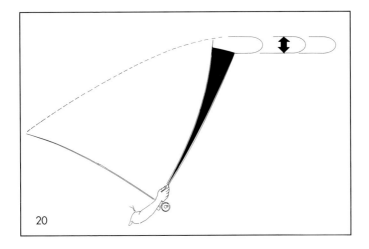

20

2. *The faster that the tip is moved through that acceleration period, and the more abruptly it is stopped, the greater the line speed.*

3. *The direction of the acceleration and stop determines the direction in which the line and fly will travel.*

As you practice, if you will keep these points in mind you will improve your fly casting technique dramatically.

A TOOL THAT WILL HELP YOU FORM BETTER LOOPS

ILLUSTRATION 21 — The most difficult part of fly casting is developing a long rod sweep, followed by a quick acceleration and stop in the correct direction. Of course it takes a fair amount of work space to practice this technique, and many people do not have convenient access to a large enough place for them to practice. Here is an easy way to make a tool that I have designed for practicing casting in confined spaces.

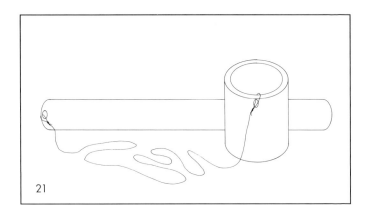

21

From a plumbing supply house or hardware store, purchase one foot of 3/4-inch plastic pipe and a one-inch plastic pipe coupling. Total cost of the two items should be less than $3.00. Secure four feet of fairly strong cord, about 1/8-inch in diameter. Parachute cord is ideal.

Drill a hole in one end of the pipe and another in the end of the coupling of sufficient size so that you can run the cord through the hole. Attach one end of the cord to the hole in each drilled piece.

ILLUSTRATION 22 — If you want to improve the acceleration stroke and stop at the end of your back cast, do this. Grasp the pipe at the base where the cord is attached in the same manner as you would hold a fly rod. Slide the coupling over the end of pipe so that the coupling lies against your hand. Now make the normal long sweep that initiates a back cast. This motion should start slowly and then gradually increase in speed. When the rod hand gets an inch or so from the end of the cast, make a very rapid and incredibly short acceleration, slightly upward in direction. Then stop as quickly as you can. If you have made the correct motion, the coupling will slide off the pipe, upwards and back-

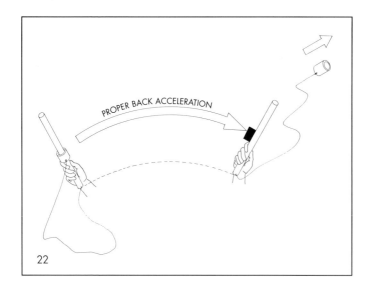

22

wards, traveling in the same path as a good back cast. Of course, a short distance behind you the cord will come taut and stop the flight of the coupling.

ILLUSTRATION 23 — To perfect your forward acceleration and stop technique, repeat this coupling casting procedure in identical fashion in the forward direction.

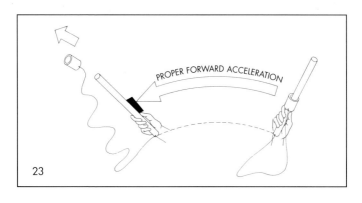

23

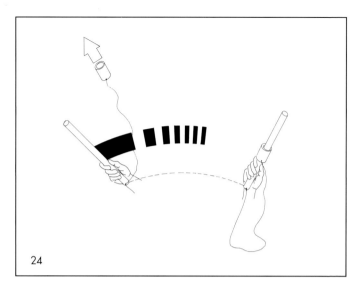

24

ILLUSTRATION 24 — This illustration shows what happens if the acceleration stroke is too long — as is the case with most fly fishermen. As shown in the illustration, if the cast is initiated and then a long acceleration is made, the coupling will slide off in an upward direction — not in the direction you would want a fly line to go toward a target. The same mistake would occur if the wrist were moved through the acceleration period.

THE CONVENTIONAL CAST

The two illustrations show the difference between the style of casting I suggest you learn and what is currently being taught by most instructors.

ILLUSTRATION 25 — The rod tip is held at about belt level (nine o'clock on the clock face).

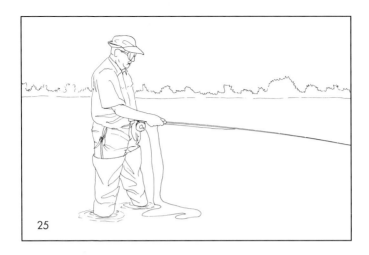

25

ILLUSTRATION 26 — The rod is brought to the near vertical position and a power stroke is made to throw the line and fly behind the angler. Then, the rod is returned to a position near where the cast was started (see Illustration 25).

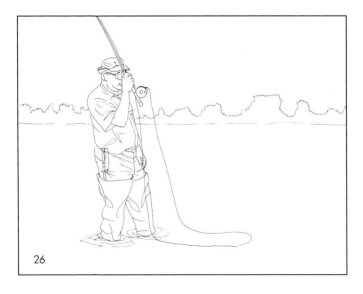

26

THE EFFECTS OF BENDING THE WRIST DURING ACCELERATION

You will recall that Principle Number Three states that the line and fly are going to go in the direction in which you accelerate and stop the rod tip at the end of the cast. And, we know that loop size is determined by the distance the rod tip is accelerated at the end of the cast.

If these factors are understood, you can then realize why bending the wrist as you accelerate the rod tip at the end of the cast is detrimental to casting technique.

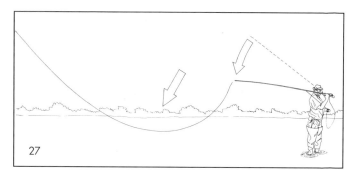

27

ILLUSTRATION 27 — If the rod is swept back to make the back cast, and at the end of that movement the wrist is rotated or bent to make the acceleration, the rod tip will travel in a long arc, ending in a downward direction behind the angler. The more the wrist is bent at the end of the cast, the farther the rod tip travels during the acceleration period and the larger the loop will be. This bending of the wrist tends to open the back cast loop and throw its energy not 180 degrees directly away from the target, but around a

Larry Kreh casting to trout on Western Run, a trout stream in central Maryland. ➤

58

curve or arc. This also results in driving some of the line down behind the angler.

Principle Number Two states that you cannot make any cast until you get the end of the line moving. But if a deep sag has been created on the back cast, much of the caster's energy being expended to move the rod tip on the forward cast really contributes nothing to driving the fly to the target. Instead, the tip must first move far enough to eliminate all slack in the line before it can begin to move the fly toward the target.

ILLUSTRATION 28 — This illustration is designed to demonstrate three points: First, since the wrist has not moved during the acceleration period, only the forearm is moving swiftly at the end of the cast. And *the direction in which the forearm and rod hand has been moved quickly and stopped is the direction in which the line is going to go.*

Second, if the angler wants to throw a tight loop behind him exactly 180 degrees directly away from the target, then the forearm and rod hand must be swept quickly in the direction shown by the arrow.

Third, because the wrist was not bent during the cast, the line travels flat and with a tight loop.

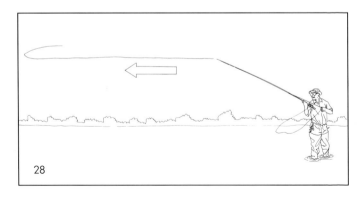

28

29

ILLUSTRATION 29 — This illustration simply shows that if the cast is to be aimed at a high angle, then during the brief acceleration period, the forearm and rod hand must travel and stop going in that direction. And, because no wrist motion was utilized, a straight line and tight loop are created.

THE DOUBLE HAUL

I find there is a good deal of confusion among fly casters about hauls and hauling technique.

As most of you probably know, a *single haul* may be described as a yank, or a jerk, or a sharp pull downwards on the line that the angler performs with his line hand while the fly line is moving through its acceleration phase on either the back or forward cast. The pulling movement is initiated with the line hand held close to the reel. When you pull swiftly on the line, it causes the rod tip to flex very fast. The faster you make the pull, the faster you move the tip. The faster the tip moves, the faster the line moves.

Many anglers use a single haul all the time when they execute their back cast. To increase line speed even more for difficult or long distance casts, some anglers also use another single haul as they execute their forward cast. When they use the two hauls on the same cast, one going back and one going forward, they've executed the *double haul*.

The major reason that most people have trouble with double hauling, I think, is that they make hauls that are too long, sometimes taking their line hand from a starting position near the reel all the way down near or behind their hip — sometimes as much as three or four feet. This looks pretty good. You see people doing it a lot. The only problem with this technique that I can think of is that it is *wrong*.

The Inefficient Double Haul

There are several reasons why anglers should not make long pulls with the line hand during the double haul: long

30

pulls on the line when double hauling are liable to create tangles and unwanted slack; they frequently tangle the line with the lower portion of the rod, often causing the line to roll outward with a resulting loss of casting energy; but most important, long pulls are inefficient. Once all the slack has been removed from the line and the rod is bent in preparation for the cast, the most efficient double haul is one in which the line hand moves only a very few inches.

ILLUSTRATION 30 — Here is a typical profile of the average angler in the process of executing the double haul with a long pull, nearly tearing off his underwear and ending up with his two hands spread apart as much as three feet.

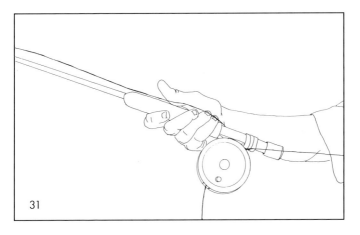

31

ILLUSTRATION 31 — Because the angler has started his cast with the thumb on top of the rod, as he reaches well behind him, he is forced to rotate his hand outward, as shown here. This rotation of the rod hand away from the body causes the line to unroll behind the angler in a wide loop that throws energy to the side, rather than straight away from the target.

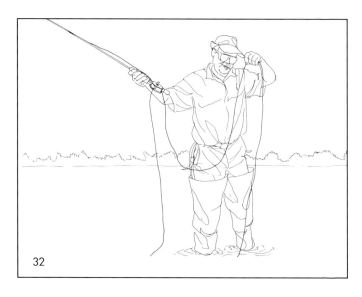

32

ILLUSTRATION 32 — With his hands spread widely apart, the caster must now bring the line hand near the rod hand so that the second pull of the double haul can be accomplished. This means pushing slack into the line. What also frequently happens is that the line tangles around the butt of the rod or becomes hooked in the reel.

Anytime the hands become widely separated during the cast, there is an excellent chance that the line will tangle with the rod butt or the reel. So even if you don't utilize the double haul technique in your casting, always try to keep your line hand within 18 inches of the rod hand at all times to avoid this problem.

Double Hauling Correctly

The haul — either the single or double haul — accomplishes only one thing in casting. It causes the line to go faster during the cast. Because of the force of gravity, a fly line begins to fall toward the water as soon as it straightens out or finishes unrolling. You can readily see this for yourself by making a few casts. Make a short cast and you'll see that as soon as the line straightens out it will start dropping. Make a longer cast and the principle remains the same: as soon as the line straightens out, the line falls.

While double hauls make the line travel faster and farther, for most anglers a double haul allows them only to throw their casting mistakes faster and farther! While such casters may obtain more distance than they could without the haul, they are not really casting better. The double haul is simply permitting them to develop greater line speed.

There are many fly fishermen who throw a fairly long line, but they do it with very poor rod hand technique. They have been able to develop their double haul so efficiently that most of the effectiveness of their cast is being produced by their double haul. But these casters are using the double haul as a crutch, not as a tool.

There's a much better way to do it. Let me show you how.

What is essential to becoming a good caster is first to learn good rod technique, and then to learn the double haul. For only after you have learned good rod hand technique does the double haul become a valuable tool.

The most important point to realize about double hauling is that *very brief and short line pulls* are essential to getting the most out of the double haul. The faster you pull on the line, the greater the tip speed. But even if you make an incredibly fast pull with the line hand, if you make a long haul, you will not be allowing the rod tip to stop abruptly. *It is critical to understand that a long pull does not allow the rod tip to stop until you have stopped pulling on the line.*

Ideally, when making a double haul, the line and the rod hand should move during the acceleration period *over the same distance*. If the rod hand accelerates four inches on the cast, the double haul should move only four inches. If the rod hand moves four inches and the line hand moves over a longer distance, the rod tip will not stop abruptly and line speed will be lost. This is a very important point in double hauling and is misunderstood by most fly casters.

Properly used, the double haul is a most valuable casting tool. With correct hauling technique, on those occasions when you make a poor cast, by double hauling you can correct much of the deficiency of the cast. Or if you need to throw an extra heavy fly or drive a fly into a stiff wind, the double haul is a wonderful casting tool.

The following illustrations do two things: they will show you how to make an efficient double haul and how to learn proper double hauling technique.

The problem that most people have when they are first learning the double haul is that too much is going on at one time. But the method explained in these illustrations allows the caster to break the double haul down into small segments so it becomes much easier to understand. Using this method, most of my students have been able to learn the rudiments of the double haul in less than 30 minutes.

ILLUSTRATION 33 — Lower the rod tip until it is near the surface and remove all slack line.

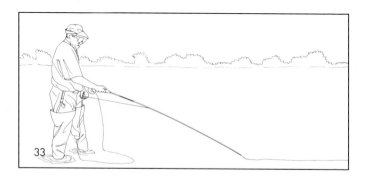

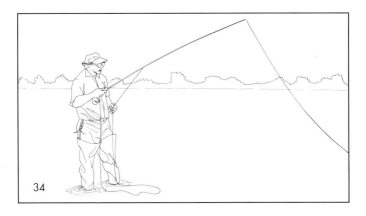

ILLUSTRATION 34 — Raise *both* hands to lift the line and get it moving and off the surface, so that you can make the proper back cast.

ILLUSTRATION 35 — When you have decided to make the acceleration and stop on your back cast, if you accelerate and stop the rod hand over a six-inch distance, then the line hand should move only over this same distance. *The line hand should jerk swiftly on the line only the same distance the rod hand has moved!* The faster the line hand moves over that distance, and the quicker that the line hand stops pull-

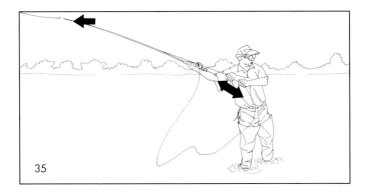

ing, the greater the line speed. When the line hand finishes the pull downward, bring it up a few inches toward the reel. This will keep the hands close together so that no slack accumulates in the line before the forward cast is made.

Again keeping the hands closely together, repeat this routine exactly in reverse on the forward cast.

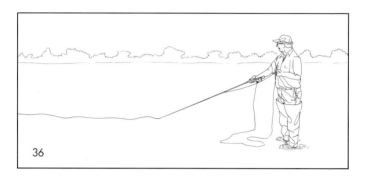

ILLUSTRATION 36— This illustration shows the method I have used quite successfully in helping my students to learn the double haul. Instead of making an immediate back cast, turn your body slightly to the rear and allow the line to fall to the grass or water behind you. When learning the double haul, dropping the line behind you in this manner gives you time to think about what you are going to do next.

ILLUSTRATION 37— Bring the rod hand and line hand forward, held rather closely together as shown in the illustration. Don't move the line hand faster. The two hands should come forward almost as if there were a bar locking them together.

ILLUSTRATION 38— At the moment that the rod hand accelerates, the line hand should accelerate or jerk on the line for the same short distance. Then as soon as the line

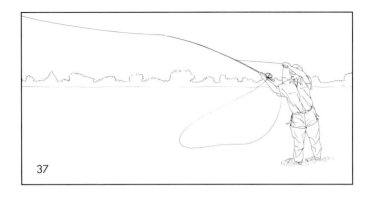

37

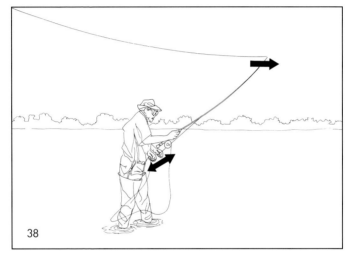

38

hand makes its jerk, allow it to bounce back a few inches as the line is traveling toward the target out in front of you. This will allow you either to make another false cast using the hauls, or in a real fishing situation to go ahead and complete your forward cast.

Important: *during this exercise or in an actual fishing situation, your two hands should remain within 18 inches of each other at all times.*

39

ILLUSTRATION 39 — This illustration simply shows a front view of Illustration 38. Note that the double arrow indicates the brief down and up motion that the line hand makes to complete the second segment of the double haul.

ROLL CASTING

The *roll cast* is employed when there is not sufficient room behind the angler to make an aerial back cast. In these circumstances, since the line cannot be thrown behind the angler, it should instead be drawn back in a certain manner, using a certain technique, until some of it falls behind the caster. Then a forward sweep of the rod rolls the line and fly toward the target. I will be explaining what I think that certain technique should be.

But first, I'd like to comment on the faulty roll casting method I frequently see anglers using — which unfortunately has now come to be accepted by many people as the conventional way to roll cast — which results in a very poor cast that usually ends with a cluttered mess of line collapsed around the fly on the water.

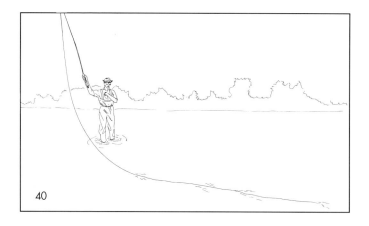

40

The Conventional Roll Cast

ILLUSTRATION 40 — With the conventional roll cast, most of the problems are created by poor technique at the very initiation of the cast. The average angler brings the rod back until it is stopped in a vertical position, often with the rod hand held in front of his body, as demonstrated in this illustration.

ILLUSTRATION 41 — The rod is then swept forward and almost always ends with the rod tip driving down toward the water in front of the angler.

Two other mistakes are also generally made on the roll cast by most casters:

First, for some peculiar reason — perhaps because they lack confidence in their ability on this particular cast — on the roll cast many anglers tend to break their wrist more often than on other types of casts, although (as I've stated previously) I do not believe you should break the wrist on any cast. Keeping in mind that the direction in which the rod tip is accelerated and stopped is the direction in which the line and fly will travel, if the wrist is used there is a tendency to drive downward at the end of the cast. By direct-

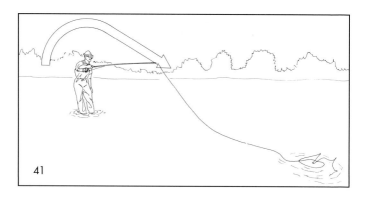

41

ing the rod tip downward, the angler is forcing the line to collapse in front of him.

Another common roll casting error is the angler's failure to pause upon the completion of the back cast to give the fly line sufficient time for the surface tension of the water to momentarily grip it, as the rod needs something to pull against when the forward cast is made. But most people don't give their fly line this opportunity.

Roll Casting Correctly

Several things should be understood before making any roll cast. The most important point is: *the forward roll cast is made exactly like you would make a normal forward cast.* The only difference between normal casting technique and roll casting technique is that the back cast is different! If you do nothing else but keep this in mind, you will improve your roll casting.

Several other points also need to be considered.

The more help you need on a cast, the longer the distance that you should move the rod through the casting arc. So if you need to make a difficult or longer roll cast, simply bring the rod farther back on the back cast.

The speed with which you accelerate and stop the rod

tip at the end of the cast determines how small the loop size will be, and how fast and far the line will travel.

If you want the line to go toward the target, you must accelerate and stop going toward the target.

If you want your line to travel far and fast, you need to accelerate very fast and stop very quickly.

You see, there's really nothing new here. These are the same principles I have been discussing with you all along. *All casting principles that apply to normal casts also apply to roll casts.*

Let's now look at how easy it is to make a good roll cast.

Note: *the following illustrations pertain to roll casting with a floating line. Roll casting with sinking-tip or sinking lines is accomplished with the single water haul and double water haul techniques, which will be discussed later in the book.*

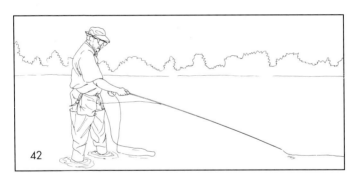

ILLUSTRATION 42 — Since you won't have the benefit of a back cast to aid you in making a good forward cast, start with the rod tip lower than normal (or near the surface).

ILLUSTRATION 43 — Gradually lift the rod (I say "slide" the line on the water toward you). Don't jerk or lift — just slowly bring the rod up and back.

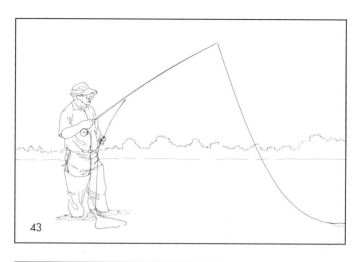

ILLUSTRATION 44 — Continue to bring the rod slowly back until it arrives at the position shown. If you need to make a longer cast, bring the rod back even a little more. The longer the rod sweeps through an arc, the more it will allow you to make difficult casts.

Then allow the line to come to a brief stop on the surface of the water. This is a vital point in roll casting technique. *You must allow the line to come to a stop!*

Remember earlier when we discussed why you should lift all line from the water before making a normal back cast? ... that because surface tension was gripping the line, to make a normal back cast, you needed to release all the line from the water before throwing the line behind you?

Well, in roll casting, you want surface tension to help you. Because when you allow the line to stop, surface tension grabs the line and gives your rod something to pull against so that it can load properly. This stopping of the line on the roll cast cannot be emphasized enough.

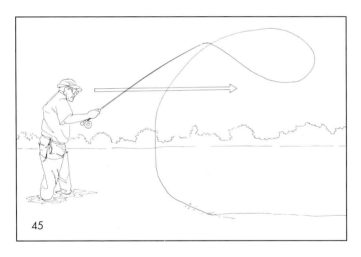

45

ILLUSTRATION 45 — As soon as the line stops, make a normal forward cast toward the target. If on a normal cast you were false casting and were ready to make a cast toward the target, at the end of the next back cast you would sweep the rod arm forward and then accelerate and stop going straight ahead toward the target. And if you wanted the line to travel swiftly and with a small loop, you would make the acceleration very fast, very short, and stop quickly in the direction of the target. Well that is precisely how you make a forward roll cast!

Remember the principal point I have been making again and again in this section: *a forward roll cast is made exactly as you would make a normal forward cast. Only the back cast is made differently.*

The Distance Roll Cast

For even moderately good casters, most roll casts are seldom made with more than about 45 feet of line outside the rod tip. That distance is considered a long roll cast. But there are occasions when a much longer one is needed, so we need to devote a little time to it.

For the long distance roll cast, all the principles we just discussed about the standard roll cast apply. What sets this cast apart from the standard roll cast is how you prepare for the forward cast with a special back cast technique.

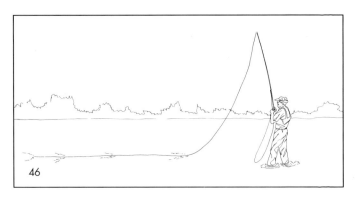

ILLUSTRATION 46 — Slide the line back on the surface by gradually elevating and raising the fly rod as you would for a standard roll cast.

47

ILLUSTRATION 47— Here is where the difference occurs. Instead of coming to a halt, as the rod reaches just beyond the vertical make a little upward rocking motion, indicated by the arrow. *Don't make a normal back cast motion.* Instead, make this curving upward motion. By lifting the rod in this manner, you'll lift much of the line directly in front of you off the water and throw it in a large loop behind you. I repeat, you are not attempting to make a back cast. You just want to deposit a considerable amount of line behind you in the attitude shown in the illustration.

ILLUSTRATION 48— The moment that the line falls to the water — *but the loop of line is still in the air* (as shown in the illustration) — begin a "climbing" forward cast. What you

48

are attempting to do here is to throw considerable line behind you, but not allow it to collapse on the surface. Then, with some line on the water (to give the rod something to pull against) you can execute the forward cast.

ILLUSTRATION 49 — Note in the illustration that the rod is directed slightly upward instead of straight ahead.

ILLUSTRATION 50 — When you feel that the rod is loaded (there is a taut pull on the line), make a normal forward cast. If everything has been performed correctly, it easy to make a roll cast from 70 to 90 feet using a weight-forward line. (Incidentally, many experts believe that using a weight-forward line hinders distance roll casting technique,

arguing that the heavier forward part of the line is difficult to pick up and roll with the thinner running line behind it.) But I assure you that for the distance roll cast, it is actually easier to obtain distance with a weight-forward line than with a double-taper line.

THE SINGLE WATER HAUL

Whenever you are using a fly line that is designed so that any portion of it sinks below the surface, you need to modify your roll casting technique. The forward cast is still made the same way as a normal forward cast. But because the line is below the surface, the angler must get the sinking line out of the water before the back cast can be made.

Many people retrieve enough line so that they can lift the sinking tip or sinking line up and out of the water with a high roll cast. Then while the line is unrolling in the air in front of them, they make their back cast. This does work, but when you make the back cast in this manner, you are pulling against air so that the rod doesn't load well. A much better way of roll casting any sinking line is to modify it with the *single water haul.* But to make this modification, you will need some room behind you. Here's the way to make the single water haul.

ILLUSTRATION 51 — Strip in enough line so that you can pick it up and make a roll cast which is *directed straight ahead in front of you.* This will cause the line to be driven in the direction shown by the arrow.

ILLUSTRATION 52 — The line will travel in the direction that the rod tip accelerates and stops. When the rod tip stops, lower it until it is very close to the surface.

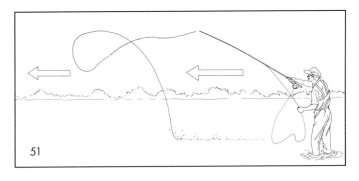

51

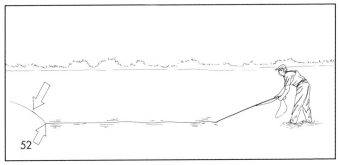

52

Watch the end of your fly line. When it unrolls and the front end of the line touches the water, you are ready to make the back cast. Don't delay, or the sinking line will sink too deeply below the surface. If you begin the back cast just as the front end of the line touches down to the surface, while you have a little of the line below the surface, you can still easily lift it.

When making the back cast, you will be in the position of leaning forward with your rod tip low and pointing at the fly. Make a long drawing-back motion with the rod. This long motion will allow you to load the rod better.

Illustration 53 — When you feel that you have properly loaded the rod, make a normal back cast. You'll be amazed

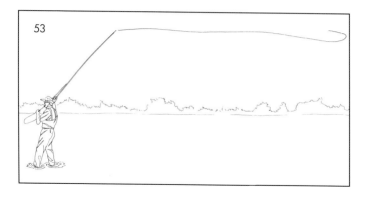

at how much better is the back cast than using the conventional method of rolling the line up in the air. Then when ready, make your forward cast.

THE DOUBLE WATER HAUL

With a sinking line, the single water haul is a great way to improve your ability to cast a long line with ease. But if you have water behind you (if you are wading or are in a boat), then the *double water haul* makes the cast even easier. This cast works especially well with sinking shooting heads, including lead core shooting head configurations.

ILLUSTRATION 54 — Bring the line up and make a roll cast so

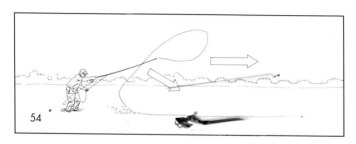

that the line straightens on the surface (just as you would when making the single water haul).

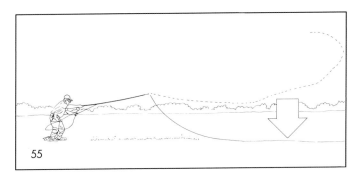

ILLUSTRATION 55 — Be sure to direct the line straight ahead and allow it to fall to the surface, just as you would with the single water haul.

ILLUSTRATION 56 — As soon as the front end of the line touches the water, make a soft or easy back cast. Make it only hard enough so that the line will straighten behind you as it falls. *Do not make a normal hard back cast!*

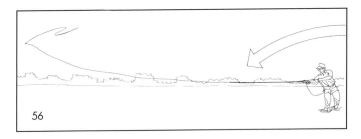

ILLUSTRATION 57 — Watch the end of the sinking line as it unrolls and begins falling. As soon as the end of the line touches down on the surface of the water, you are ready to make the forward cast.

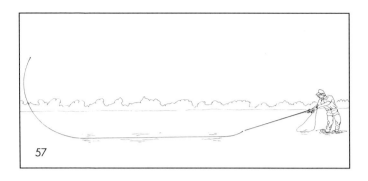

57

ILLUSTRATION 58 — The forward cast is made a little bit differently than a normal forward cast. As soon as the front end of the line touches the surface, begin a long drawing-back motion. When you feel that the rod is properly loaded, make a forward cast. Be sure to direct the forward cast at a high angle, as shown in the illustration. This high forward angle improves your ability to throw a long forward cast, and it causes the fly to travel high above your head. Anyone who has used lead core shooting heads or heavy flies carrying sharp-pointed hooks knows that it is very comforting to have the fly traveling high overhead!

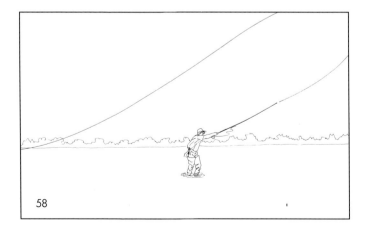

58

Use of the double water haul will allow even older people who do not possess great forearm strength to make casts with sinking shooting heads that exceed 100 feet. And there is as little effort involved in this cast as throwing a floating line 40 feet!

CASTING WITH THE WIND

Wind is said to be the enemy of the fly caster. But wind can also help you if you use it properly. Here's how to cast when the wind is at your back.

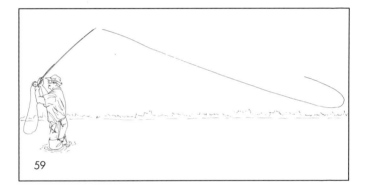

ILLUSTRATION 59 — Throw a low back cast. Try to develop as much line speed and as tight a loop as you can make. This will help straighten the back cast into the breeze.

ILLUSTRATION 60 — Since the wind will act on the fly line much as it would on a kite, throw the forward cast at least as high as the angle shown in the illustration. If you make a good back cast and an elevated forward cast, the wind can help you cast much farther than you would under calm conditions.

60

CASTING INTO THE WIND

Whenever you are casting into the wind, you have problems. One of the major problems is that once the fly line has straightened out (or has unrolled toward the target), the wind blows the straightened leader and fly back toward the angler. To cast well into the wind, the angler should throw the cast as fast as possible, with a small loop.

ILLUSTRATION 61 — With the wind blowing in your face, make a high back cast as shown in the illustration.

ILLUSTRATION 62 — When ready, make a forward cast. *But make the cast by directing the fly straight at the target*, causing the line and fly to travel toward the surface and toward the target. This is one of the very few times when a cast should be directed downward. If the cast is directed prop-

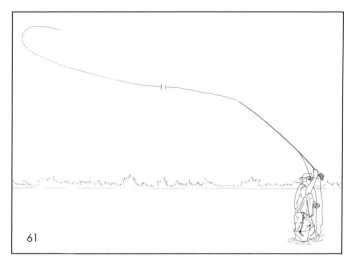

61

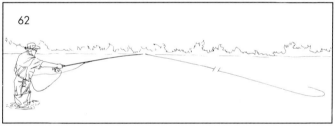

62

erly, as soon as the leader straightens out the fly will fall to the surface, preventing the line and leader from being blown backwards by the breeze.

CASTING WITH THE WIND BLOWING TO THE ROD SIDE OF THE ANGLER

One of the most troublesome casting situations you can ever confront is when the wind is blowing from the same side as the side on which you are holding your rod. In this situation, on the forward stroke the line and fly will tend to blow too close to you, possibly hooking you. Some anglers will make a backhand cast in such a situation, but that restricts body movement. What is needed is a method of casting that allows you freedom of movement and the use of normal casting strokes. The following procedure does just that.

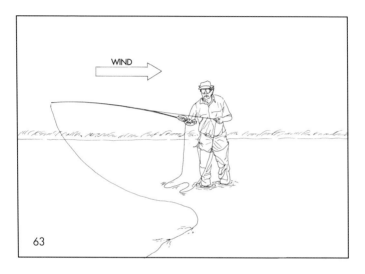

ILLUSTRATION 63 — Because the wind will blow the line in against the angler, the back cast is made to the windward side. This side cast will cause the line to flow back and well away from the caster.

ILLUSTRATION 64 — This is a side view of the forward cast. After a side cast has been made, the rod is brought up and around. *It's very important that the rod be brought through a perfectly vertical plane during the entire forward cast.*

ILLUSTRATION 65 — If the rod is brought forward in a per-

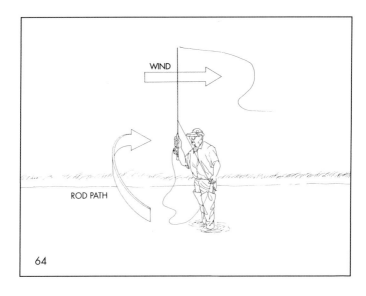

64

fectly vertical plane, and a normal forward cast is then made, the wind will blow the line to the lee side or downwind of the angler, thus missing him completely. The good thing about this cast is that you are using all normal casting motions that allow you freedom of movement.

65

THE CHANGE OF DIRECTION CAST

There are many situations where the angler must quickly change the direction of the cast. Perhaps a flats' fisherman is working a bonefish when another fish offers a better opportunity. The angler must disregard the first fish and make a quick cast to another. Or a common need for a change of direction cast occurs when the trout fisherman presents his fly upstream and allows it to drift downstream beyond him, but then wants to cast the fly back to the exact spot to which he first cast. Since the most effective fly cast will be made when the angler is able to throw his back cast in a direction 180 degrees (or exactly opposite) from the target, people who have not mastered the proper technique have to make several side-stream or upstream false casts, working progressively up the stream, until they have positioned themselves so that their back cast will travel in a direction of about 180 degrees away from their original target.

But there is a better and much more efficient way to do this which I would like to show you.

In the illustrations that follow, the angler is making a change of direction cast from his left to a point directly in front of him.

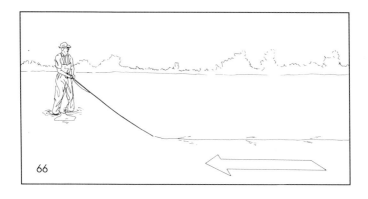

66

ILLUSTRATION 66— The angler is ready to make a cast directly in front of him. *The rod is kept as low as possible to the surface of the water* as the tip is moved fairly rapidly.

ILLUSTRATION 67— When the rod tip points directly at the target, it is time to make the back cast. It is absolutely vital that *you do not let the rod tip stop, or cease moving, during the entire cast.* Remember, Principle Number Two says you can't make a cast until you get the end of the line moving.

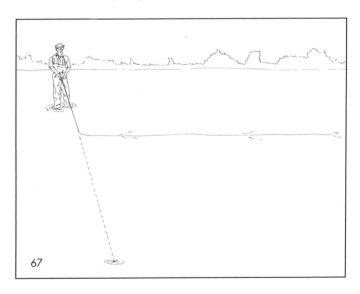

67

ILLUSTRATION 68— The rod has swept along the surface until it points at the target and at that precise moment a back cast is made in the normal manner. Because the rod was pointed at the target, and the acceleration was directly away from the target, the line will flow 180 degrees from the target. Remember, the line is going to go in the direction in which you accelerate and stop the rod tip at the end of the cast.

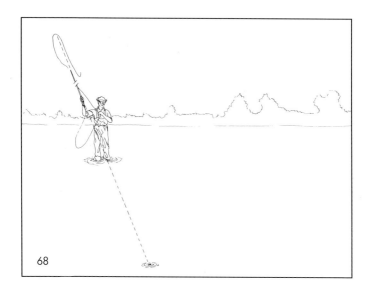

68

ILLUSTRATION 69 — As soon as the back cast unfolds behind the angler, a normal forward cast can be made. Such change of direction casts are easy to make, so long as you . . .

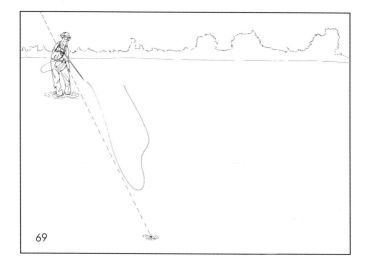

69

. . . keep the rod tip low as you move the line along the surface;

. . . don't stop moving the line at any time during the cast;

. . . only make your back cast when the rod points at the target.

CASTING WITH LITTLE ROOM BEHIND YOU

There are occasional fishing situations, particularly when seeking trout, where you need to cast a fairly long distance in front of you, but have little room behind you and where, for one reason or another, a roll cast would be inappropriate. For example, if you are standing on the bank of a stream a number of feet away from the water, the roll cast will not work because you have no water surface right at your feet to provide the surface tension on the line that is needed to load the rod properly for a roll cast.

As an alternative to the roll cast, there is a cast that is so simple and easy to master that with as little as 30 feet of room behind you, you can easily cast 50 to 70 feet in front of you.

70

ILLUSTRATION 70 — To perfect this cast, it is a good idea to first learn an exercise that will prepare you for making the real cast. Put about 10 or 12 feet of fly line outside the rod tip. Rotate the rod tip in a wide circle as shown in the illustration, but by exerting only a small amount of force against the rod as you go around the circle. When you do, the rod tip will cause the line to flow in a circle, just like a whirling lasso.

When you have mastered this technique and can keep the line circling for a minute or more, then you are ready for step two. As the rod rotates around to a position vertical to you, make a sharp forward cast. Because you have been pulling on the line, it is tight, and you'll find that you can make a fairly acceptable forward cast.

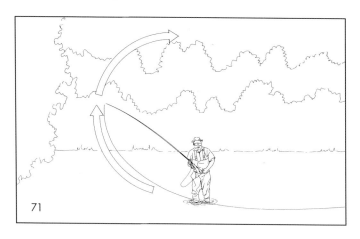

71

ILLUSTRATION 71 — Now you are ready to make the actual cast. Sweep the rod in a circle, applying pressure during the area of the cast shown by the arrows in the illustration.

ILLUSTRATION 72 — When the rod reaches a vertical plane, make a sharp forward cast by accelerating and stopping

72

quickly toward the target. If you can make a single haul, it will assist you in making an even better cast.

THE RIGHT ANGLE CAST

So many times, especially when trout fishing, you will be confronted with a situation where there is an obstruction directly opposite your casting side, and yet you want to throw your fly at a right angle to that obstruction. Up to about 35 feet, such a cast is easy. Beyond that distance, if you attempted to take the rod back at 180 degrees directly away from the target to execute a normal back cast, you would be casting into the obstruction. To overcome this problem, you should execute a right angle cast. Here's how to do it.

ILLUSTRATION 73 — In this illustration, trees are along the left side and close to you. You make a back cast behind you in the normal way.

73

74

ILLUSTRATION 74 — Because you want some help on this cast, extend your arm well behind your body. When you initiate your forward cast, draw your rod hand forward as if you were going to cast directly in front of you.

ILLUSTRATION 75 — *Note the path of the arrow.* That is the exact path your rod hand should travel. When the rod hand

75

is in front of your face, turn your hand toward the right-angle target. Do not accelerate the rod until *after* the rod hand is fully turned toward the target.

ILLUSTRATION 76 — As soon as the rod hand is turned toward the target, make a short, fast acceleration and stop. The fly line will flow from along the tree line behind you, then make a right angle turn and deposit the fly at the target.

76

hand so that a retrieve can be started just as soon as the fly hits the water.

Illustration 77 — Here is the wrong way to do it. Note in the illustration that the angler's line hand is empty! After they shoot a lot of line toward the target, most fishermen simply abandon the line completely. This is a mistake I see fly fisherman make very often, even those who are pretty good casters. It is a mistake for at least two reasons. First, abandoned line that flows in this manner toward the target approaches the stripping guide wavering wildly, frequently overwrapping the rod guide, or worse, tangling in the reel or around the butt of the rod. And second, releasing the line as it shoots through the guides means a total loss of control during the cast.

Illustration 78 — The proper way to control the line on the shoot is to allow it to flow through a large "O" ring formed by the thumb and first finger of the line hand, as

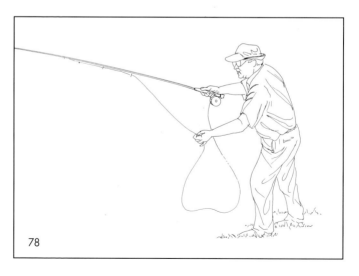

78

CONTROLLING LINE ON THE SHOOT

At the end of the cast, after the line has been released and shot through the rod guides toward the target, with good line control technique the angler can very rapidly retrieve part of the line, pick it up, make a back and forward cast, and then shoot the line a second time back out to the target. But he cannot do this if he has abandoned the line. He must instead control it.

This is a particularly important technique to develop for saltwater casting, where you are frequently confronted with fast moving fish whose timetable does not include waiting around in the area for you to get your act together and make a second cast to them.

But it has many fresh water applications also. If the line is not abandoned, but is kept under your control, it can be stopped over the target, or be brought back under the rod

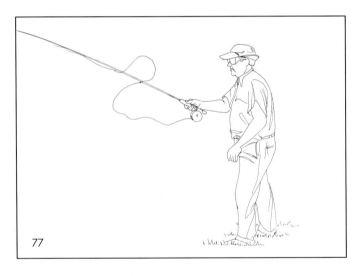

77

OVERLEAF: *Dave Whitlock, one of the modern masters, at work.*

demonstrated in the illustration. When line is allowed to flow through the "O" ring in this manner, it never tangles in the guide or around the reel or butt section. This technique allows the angler to stop the line's flight at his discretion; and it also gives him the ability to then place the line under the rod hand so that an instant retrieve or strike can be made as soon as the fly alights.

In employing this technique, it is important never to release line in the hand until the acceleration and stop on the forward cast has occurred.

CONTROLLING LINE WHEN WADING

While wading or standing in flowing water, a most frustrating fly fishing situation is trying to control line that has been retrieved and is lying on the water, tangling underfoot and restricting casting. Here is a method to eliminate this problem.

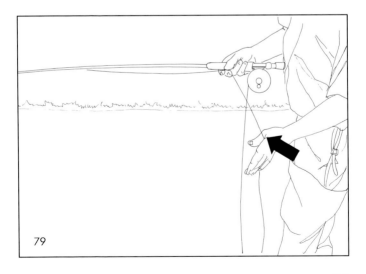

79

ILLUSTRATION 79 — Generally, 10 or 12 feet of line can be retrieved before problems arise. After you have recovered about 10 or 12 feet of line, as you are making your retrieve place a loop of this line between the thumb and first finger as shown in the illustration.

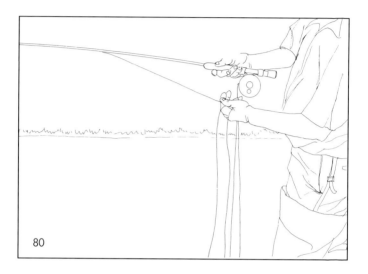

80

ILLUSTRATION 80 — As soon as this first loop of line has been trapped between the thumb and the first finger, grasp the line with the end of the thumb and first finger and retrieve more line. When another 10 or 12 feet have been retrieved, loop and clamp it between the thumb and first finger, *but forward or in front of the first loop you are holding.* If necessary, you can retrieve one more loop and hold it between the thumb and the finger. But always be sure that each loop is trapped in front of the one before it.

This technique will allow you to recover as much as 30 feet of line. If you are wading in a trout stream, stand still and get ready to make another cast. If you are wading on a bonefish flat, simply carry the line as you walk.

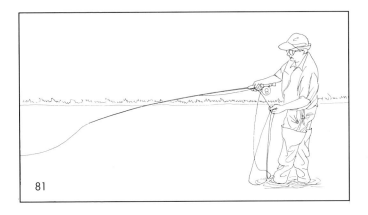

81

ILLUSTRATION 81 — When ready for the next cast, lower the rod, remove all slack, and begin a normal back cast.

ILLUSTRATION 82 — Because the two or three loops are firmly held between the thumb and first finger, you can handle the line at the tip of the finger and thumb and make a normal cast. In this illustration, the angler is beginning the forward cast and the loops are easily under his control.

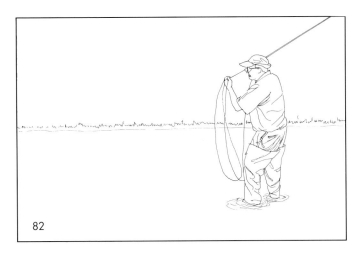

82

ILLUSTRATION 83 — As soon as acceleration stops on the forward cast, the line hand opens, as shown in the illustration.

ILLUSTRATION 84 — This is a wider view as the angler releases the line. With a little practice, a wading angler can retrieve 30 or more feet of line, hold it in loops, make a back cast, come forward and shoot the entire line (tangle-free) to the target.

There are numerous fishing situations where the ability to lift a lot of line from the water and make a good cast is essential to success. But most fishermen have problems picking up a long line. The major reason why is surface tension. Surface tension is grasping the fly line and doesn't want to release it from the water. But once the line is free of the surface, a relatively long cast can be made by almost anyone with even moderate skills.

85

ILLUSTRATION 85 — There are a few essential steps you need to take to get the line free from the surface. You will recall Principle Number One states that the more help you need on the cast, the more you move the rod through a longer

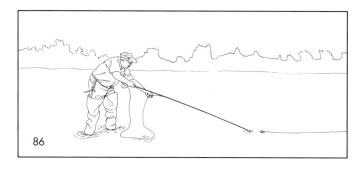

86

arc. So where you need help to pick up a long line, start the cast with the rod tip actually an inch below the surface.

ILLUSTRATION 86 — Strip in line until all slack has been removed. *Note that the line hand is almost touching the first rod guide. The line hand should remain in this position as the rod is lifted.*

87

ILLUSTRATION 87 — Raise the butt section of the rod first, and without stopping, raise the rod tip. Don't do this too slowly or the line between the rod tip and the water will sag and make the cast more difficult. But don't raise it too rapidly or you'll be ripping the line off the surface of the water, losing casting energy. *Note that during the lifting process, the hand holding the line has remained right where you started, close to the first guide.*

ILLUSTRATION 88 — When you have lifted all the line that you possibly can through the action of raising the rod, then

88

make a long pull with the line hand. This should allow you to lift all remaining line from the surface. *Look intently at the end of your fly line. When it is free of the surface, make your back cast, using a single haul.*

THE BASEBALL THROW CAST

For throwing a tight loop, or casting into the wind, or casting straight back under an overhanging obstacle, no other cast approaches this one for effectiveness, at least as far as I am concerned. For lack of a better name, I've been calling it the *baseball throw cast*. The key to this cast is how you end up the acceleration at the end of the forward cast. Here's how you go about it.

ILLUSTRATION 89 — Make a good back cast, reaching as far back as possible. A straight arm like this aids in making a better baseball throw cast.

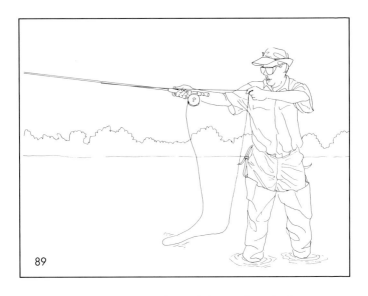

89

ILLUSTRATION 90 — Bring the rod forward with the tip *parallel to the surface*. Don't allow the tip to rise as it would in normal casting. Instead, now shove the rod butt forward, directly at the target.

ILLUSTRATION 91 — When the shoulders are in the position shown in the illustration, *the forearm should be horizontal and moving parallel to the surface of the water.*

90

91

ILLUSTRATION 92 — Principle Number Three states that the fly and line are going to go in the direction in which the rod tip is accelerated and stopped at the end of the cast. Note the direction of the arrow. This indicates that you should stab or jab the rod as fast as you can, straight ahead over a very short distance. Because you are going straight ahead, it's also easy to stop quickly. This procedure will give you a very tight loop, insuring that almost all of your casting energy is going straight toward the target. But note that if you jab at a downward or upward angle, the line will not go straight, but down or up.

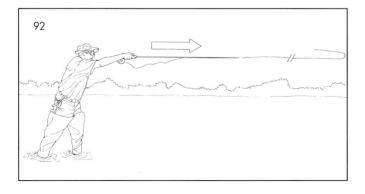

92

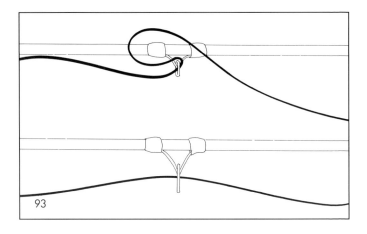

ILLUSTRATION 93 — The size of your stripping guide has a great deal to do with how well you shoot line on the forward cast. This is because when you shoot a line through a fly rod guide, it doesn't come up and sneak smoothly through the guide. Instead, if there is any speed on the shoot, the line comes up in wildly wavering waves, often doubling over the rod guide, as shown at the top of this illustration.

Almost all fly fishermen who can throw a fast line will occasionally experience their line overlapping the stripping guide and snagging around the rod guide. But once the line enters the stripping or butt guide, it will travel in a straight line. Thus, the size of the stripping guide is a major factor in shooting a longer line effectively.

Proper stripping guide size is obviously critical in such fly fishing situations as steelheading or saltwater fly fishing,

Angler casting to largemouth bass in the Rim Canal of Lake Okeechobee in Florida. ➤

where long shoots are common. But it is just as important in trout fishing, where because you rarely have a lot of fly line outside the rod tip, when you do want to shoot line even a short distance, you have so little weight (or an amount of line) outside the rod tip that you need all the help you can get, and a larger stripping guide does help.

Manufacturers are fully aware that a larger stripping guide results in better shooting line performance. But apparently they have determined that from a cosmetic standpoint, the larger stripping guide is simply not as pleasing to the eye as a smaller one, so for retail sales they generally equip their rods with a smaller guide.

To eliminate or at least reduce the problem, I suggest that you install a larger butt or stripping guide. If you don't know how to do it, almost any fly shop can handle the chore for you.

After years of experimenting, here are my recommendations for stripping guide sizes. If you use any trout rod throwing a line size from 1 through 6, I suggest the smallest guide be a 12 mm. And if you can stand it use a 16 mm. guide, you'll get a little more edge. If you use a rod that throws a line heavier than size 6, the absolute minimum size is 16 mm., and a 20 or 22 mm. is much better. In fact, when using lines from size 10 through 13, a size 22 mm. is definitely recommended.

THROWING AN EXTRA-HIGH BACK CAST

ILLUSTRATION 94 — There are many casting situations where there is an obstruction behind the angler, but if a high back cast can be made, the obstruction can be avoided. Principle Number Three states that the line and fly are going in the direction in which you accelerate and stop the rod tip at the

94

end of the cast. But when you hold the rod in a normal position, with the thumb on the backside of the handle from the target, you are unable to make a very high back cast because the hand is actually traveling toward the object you want to avoid.

To get set up for this cast, then, turn the rod hand upside down (as shown in the circle within the illustration) and you can make your rod stop and not be going toward the obstruction.

Initiate the cast with the thumb underneath as shown in the illustration, and with the rod tip an inch under water. Remove all slack between the rod tip and the line. Now look at the obstruction behind you.

ILLUSTRATION 95 — You cannot make your first back cast until the end of the line is moving and off the surface of the water. But if you will raise your rod hand higher than your head, as shown in the illustration, you'll find that all your line will break free of the surface and you can complete the back cast.

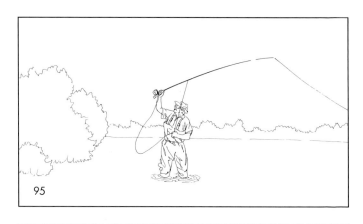

95

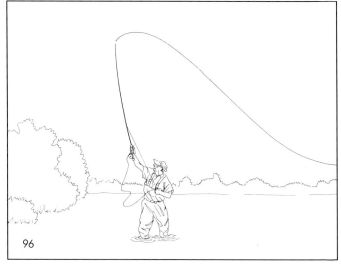

96

ILLUSTRATION 96 — The line is going to go in the direction in which you accelerate and stop the rod tip. Concentrate on making the acceleration and stop so that you avoid the obstruction. Note that the thumb is on the side of the caster — not on the side of the obstruction — when the rod tip is accelerated.

97

ILLUSTRATION 97 — As soon as the acceleration and stop occurs behind you, turn the rod hand around so that you can make a normal forward cast.

ILLUSTRATION 98 — Sweep the rod forward until you feel that you can make a forward cast.

98

ILLUSTRATION 99 — When everything feels right, make a cast toward the target.

SHOOTING HEAD TRICKS

A *shooting head* (or shooting taper, as it is also called), is a heavier forward portion of fly line, to which a long length of much thinner "shooting line" is attached. Using a line rigged up this way, when a final forward cast is made, releasing the heavier head, it travels a great deal farther than a conventional fly line because the thinner shooting line is so much easier to drag toward the target.

When a cast is made with a conventional fly line, as you sweep forward or backward, the line is straight. When the rod stops at the end of the acceleration, the line immediately outside the rod tip folds over and begins unrolling toward the target.

The shooting head has such a thin line immediately behind the head that if too much of this thin line is extended outside the rod tip, as the rod stops, the thin line collapses. The shooting line is not thick enough to unroll smoothly and drags the heavier head along behind it. The amount of the thin shooting line attached to the rear of the shooting head that is held outside the rod tip during the cast is called *overhang*.

To make long casts, it is important to get a fair amount of overhang outside the handle, but not too much.

The proper amount of overhang that will be extended beyond the rod tip varies with each fly rod outfit and the angler using it. That is, what works for me, maybe won't work for you, or vice versa. So, everyone has to determine for himself what is the proper amount of overhang he can handle for the casting outfit he is using. Fortunately, there is an easy method of doing this.

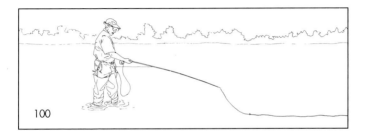

ILLUSTRATION 100 — Lower the rod and remove all slack from the line.

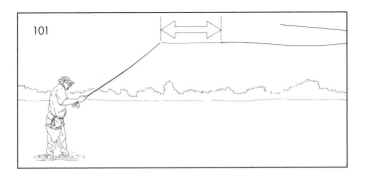

ILLUSTRATION 101 — Begin false casting with about two feet of line outside the rod tip (two feet of overhang). Look at the shooting head and you will note that the line is unrolling smoothly, as shown in the illustration.

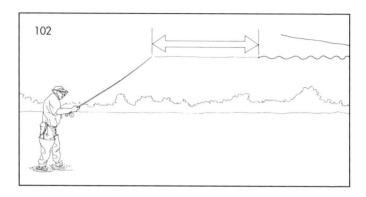

ILLUSTRATION 102 — Continue to false cast, but slowly extend more overhang. The moment that you see a series of small line humps or waves in the cast, you have reached a point where you are now putting out too much overhang. Often, this is only an additional distance of a foot or two.

ILLUSTRATION 103 — Continue to false cast, but gradually reduce the amount of overhang. As soon as the waves or

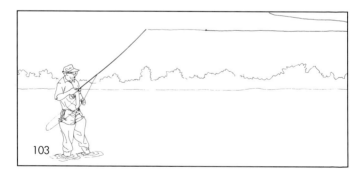

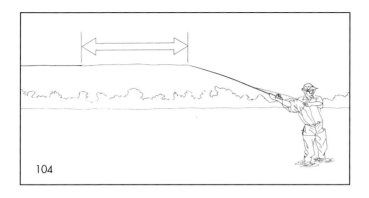

104

humps disappear, you have established what is the proper amount of overhang for you with the particular casting outfit you are using. Remember, the amount of overhang will differ from angler to angler and from outfit to outfit.

ILLUSTRATION 104 — I don't know why this is, but when you are ready to make the final forward cast you can add yards of distance by trying this tip. On only the last back cast, shoot about as much line as you have out for the overhang. In other words, if you were able to handle six feet of overhang and false cast a smooth line, then shoot an additional six feet on the final back cast. A caution: *you can only shoot this line on the last back cast.* Then come forward and shoot the head. It will go a considerable distance.

THE SPEED CAST

Anyone who has fished for bonefish, permit or tarpon from the casting platform of a flats boat, waiting for a fish to appear, knows you must be ready to cast at all times. Such fish are generally moving and you have very little time to get the line in the air and make a good cast. You can't drag the line in the water alongside the boat, for the fly will snag on the bottom or on drifting grass and debris.

You need to be able to hold enough line and the fly outside the rod tip so that you can make a cast rather quickly when the quarry is seen. I call this the *speed cast*, and the following illustrations will demonstrate how to do it.

In executing this cast, what you should keep foremost in your thinking is that you should never rush, but only make the speed cast as quickly as it is comfortable for you. And second, how you hold the fly, the line, and the rod, are the keys to success.

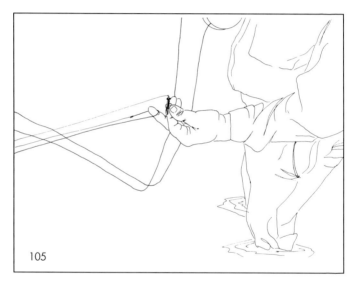

105

ILLUSTRATION 105 — Pull off enough line so that the leader and about 15 feet of fly line are outside the rod tip. About a foot or two behind the leader and fly line connection, lay that fly line over the second finger of your line hand, as shown in the illustration. Then pinch the fly very lightly between the thumb and first finger.

106

ILLUSTRATION 106 — *How you hold the line in the rod hand is critical.* Hold it exactly as shown in the illustration, with the line going under the *second* finger. If you do this, you'll see that there is a space between the hand and the rod.

107

ILLUSTRATION 107 — When a fish is seen, make a back cast 180 degrees from the fish.

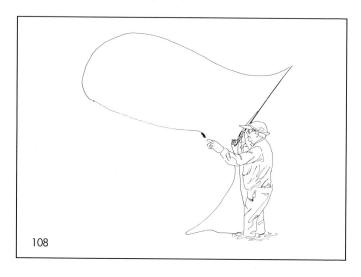

108

ILLUSTRATION 108 — The back cast should be made rather hard, so that *it actually pulls the fly from the pinched thumb and finger.* If you have pinched the fly tightly enough for the fly to be pulled from the fingers, the tension created by this fly-pull gives the rod something to load against so that a good back cast can be made. *But do not release the fly from the fingers and throw it into the air and then make a back cast,* for if you do, the rod has nothing to pull against and it becomes much more difficult to load it.

ILLUSTRATION 109 — At the same time that the line is unrolling on the back cast, the line hand moves over and grasps the line immediately in front of the rod handle. If the line has been held in the rod hand under the second finger, there will be a space between the rod and line, so the hand can quickly slip in and grasp it.

109

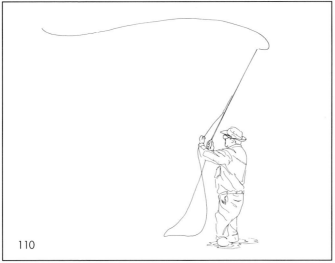

110

ILLUSTRATION 110 — A forward cast is made toward the target. If the cast is very short, the fly can be presented to the fish. But if a longer cast needs to be made, another back cast, combined with a single haul, allows you to shoot line on the back cast.

111

ILLUSTRATION 111 — Note that the two hands are kept close together for efficient casting. Don't get the hands spread too far apart or you may encounter slack that can spoil the cast.

ILLUSTRATION 112 — When you feel that another forward cast is needed, release the line toward the target.

112

Picture this situation: while standing on the boat platform waiting for a fish to appear, you are holding the line and loops in your hand. But since there is a breeze, the loops of your line are blowing around and becoming entangled, making a speed cast impossible. What do you do?

Captain Flip Pallot, of Homestead, Florida, showed me a neat trick that keeps the line under control and also prevents it from tangling.

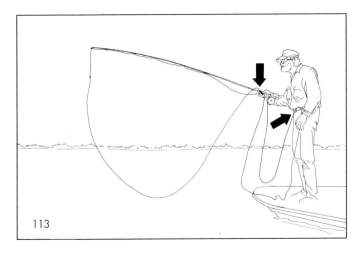

113

ILLUSTRATION 113 — It is the line coming off the reel that frequently tangles with a loop of line as the wind works against both segments of the line. Flip tucks the line coming off the reel lightly under the belt of his pants, as shown in the illustration. This spreads apart the line coming off the reel from any loops held by the angler.

ILLUSTRATION 114 — When the speed cast is made, ignore the line tucked under the belt, and concentrate on the fish.

114

Sweep the rod tip in a direction 180 degrees away from the fish. Again, as I cautioned you before, *do not release and throw the fly away*, but use the flipping action of the rod tip to pull the fly from your clenched thumb and finger, giving the rod something to work against for loading.

ILLUSTRATION 115 — If the line is correctly trapped under the second finger of the rod hand, when the back cast is

115

made there will exist a gap between the rod and the fly line. While the back cast is being made, the left hand (assuming you are right-handed) can be inserted between the rod and line to grab the line, so that you are now in a normal false casting position.

116

Illustration 116 — If a long back cast is made, you may come forward and make the forward cast to the target. If not, you are in position to make additional false casts and shoot line on each one until you believe you have sufficient line out to present the fly to the target.

After you have practiced it a bit, you will find that this technique will allow you to make a presentation to even a distant target in less than six seconds.

THE MOST COMMON CASTING MISTAKES

Based upon my experience in teaching fly casting professionally for over 35 years, if I were asked to identify the most common mistakes that I see most frequently among fly casters at the beginner and intermediate levels of ability, it would be these five:

1. *Initiating the back cast with the rod tip held too high.*
2. *For a number of reasons that I have discussed, creating a big sag in the line on the back cast.*
3. *Using too much wrist motion near the end of the back and forward casts.*
4. *Casting too hard.*
5. *Casting with the elbow held too high.*

While the first four mistakes on the list have already been examined in some detail in the book, I would now like to discuss the fifth mistake: casting with the elbow held too high; and as well review another mistake that I frequently see even very experienced fly casters having a problem with: tailing loops.

Raising The Elbow Too High

ILLUSTRATION 117 — Some anglers feel that when a high back cast is called for, they should elevate their arm and elbow above their shoulder and maintain it in that high position throughout most of the cast. This can lead to many casting problems, the principal one being the creation of a tailing loop.

ILLUSTRATION 118 — There are other ways to create a tailing loop on the cast, as I will be explaining below, but the reason a tailing loop is created when the elbow is held too high is that when the elbow is raised as high as, or even higher than the arm, there is a tendency on the part of the caster on his forward cast to bring the arm forward in the same

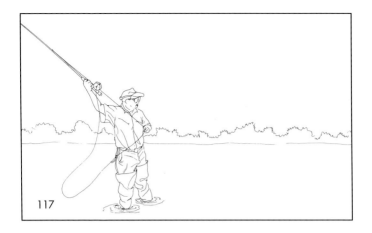

117

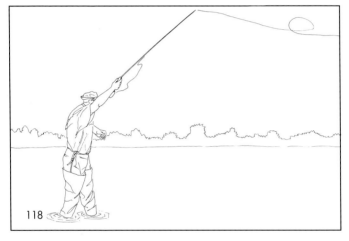

118

path that it traveled on the back cast. This causes the line to return on the same plane, and a tailing loop results, as is illustrated here.

Remember, it is not how high that you hold the arm or elbow that determines how high the back cast will go. It is the direction in which you accelerate and stop the rod tip at the end of the back cast.

Tailing Loops

Perhaps the most frustrating problem for anyone who is moderately skilled in the art of fly casting is what we call a *tailing loop*. The tailing loop is created on the forward cast. It may be described as what happens when the upper part of the loop in the line drops down near the end of the forward cast and tangles with the leader, creating a knot there.

Many casters call these knots in their leader "wind knots." I call them bad casting knots. I assure you that many people get them all the time even when there is no wind!

Videos and books have blamed all sorts of things on tailing loops and "wind knots." These range from casting too soon to casting too late. But these are not the reasons.

There are several very rare and uncommon ways a tailing loop may be created. One is when you throw a back cast that is so weak that it dies as it falls behind you. This line sometimes creates a tailing loop as it comes forward. Another is when you throw a line so weakly in front of you that it falls or collapses or fails. (I really don't call this a tailing loop, but rather a dying or collapsing cast.) Another is when you cast a line so vigorously that it creates a shock wave in the line, which in turn ends up creating an upside down roll cast and possibly, a tailing loop. But these very rare casting errors are responsible, I believe, for only about one percent of all tailing loops.

The remaining 99 percent — 99 percent! — of all tailing loops are created by only one thing: by the caster driving the line straight ahead at the end of the forward cast, without doing anything else.

◄ *Angler casting on the Beaverkill River, a famous trout stream in New York state.*

Anytime that you make a cast — keeping in mind that the line is going to go in the direction in which you accelerate and stop the rod tip — if you make your stop going straight ahead you will get a tailing loop.

Compare this to the game of pool. On the pool table, when you hit a numbered ball with the cue ball in a straight line which drives the numbered ball against one of the side rails, if you don't do anything else to change the path or plane of the cue ball, when the numbered ball caroms off the rail, because it is in the same plane with the cue ball, it will crash into it. This is exactly what happens with a tailing loop. The line is actually crashing into itself.

Some people say you will get a tailing loop if you stop too soon in the cast. But stopping too soon is not the problem, rather it is that you have shoved the line straight ahead too early. You see, it is not when you do something in the cast, it's the fact that you stopped going straight ahead.

For example, I have observed some pretty good fly casters follow this sort of routine. They'll first make two false casts, and then wind up to throw that hummer clear across the river on the next cast. And to do this, on their final forward cast they aggressively reach way out and push the rod straight ahead, creating a tailing loop in their line. They did not tail their false casts, because they didn't reach straight out in front on the false casts. But on the final cast they tailed their line because to achieve additional distance on the cast, they reached so far out in front of their body that they were forced *to stop their rod going straight ahead.*

A simpler way of explaining how to avoid tailing loops would be to say that you should put the bottom of your fly line on the bottom of the loop, and the top of your fly line on the top. To get rid of tailing loop problems is really as simple as that, if you understand the principles involved. Perhaps these next two illustrations will help.

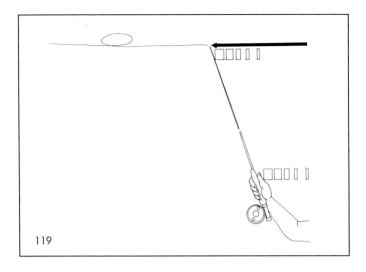

119

ILLUSTRATION 119 — As explained before, when the rod hand accelerates and stops going directly ahead, the force is directed at the target. Of course, this is exactly what you want to do, since stopping in any other direction means throwing the cast somewhere other than at the target. But if you don't do something else, your line is going to be directed straight ahead and a tailing loop will be the result.

ILLUSTRATION 120 — Instead, what you want to do is *dip the rod tip slightly, immediately after the forward cast ends.* The *instant* the rod stops its acceleration toward the target, the tip should be dipped a distance no more than what I call a "frog's hair." If you drop the rod tip too much you will open your loop and reduce the distance of the cast.

To properly execute this movement, as soon as the rod tip stops, tilt the thumb downward just enough for you to be aware that it has moved. Remember, an 1/8-inch movement at the rod hand transmits into more than a foot of movement at the rod tip.

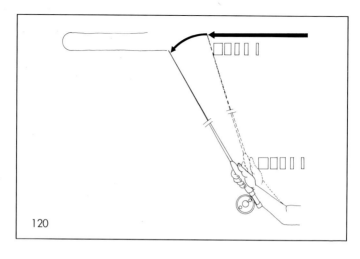

If you will learn this simple trick of *dropping the tip very slightly* as soon as your forward rod stop occurs, you will eliminate the tailing loop problem.

THREE OTHER COMMON MISTAKES

While not on my "top five" list of common casting mistakes made by casters at the beginning and intermediate levels of ability, or my "top six" if you also want to include the tailing loop mistake that is often a problem for more experienced fly casters, I would like to point out three other casting mistakes which need to be omitted from your technique:

Pulling the Loop Apart

On the forward cast, a common mistake made by many casters is that after they have completed their acceleration

Chuck Edghill fishing Sherman's Creek, Pennsylvania. ➤

and stop, they immediately drop their rod tip, pulling their loop apart.

Keep in mind that the moment you stop the cast as you come forward, a loop is beginning to form in your line at the rod tip. If you immediately drop the rod tip, you will pull the bottom of the loop away from the top, thus enlarging the size of the loop to the point that it detracts from the effectiveness of your cast.

Of course, in many fishing situations, there are times when you will want to drop your rod tip upon completion of the cast.

But the point I am making is that you don't want to stop your rod at the exact moment after you have made your acceleration and stop. Wait a bit.

You want to let your loop escape and unroll at least one rod length beyond the rod tip before you drop it. After you have come to the stop, if you will wait for the loop to unroll at least nine or 10 feet before you drop the rod, you'll increase your distance on the cast substantially.

Be careful not to confuse this fault with the slight downward tilt of thumb that you should use to avoid tailing loops — remember the distance of a "frog's hair?" — which of course does serve to drop the rod tip, but only slightly.

Causing the Line to Snap, Crackle or Pop

If you hear a pop, or crack, or snap when you make your forward cast, you started your forward cast too quickly, before your back cast had a chance to straighten out a sufficient distance behind you.

Straightening Out the Line Completely on the Back Cast

In making longer casts, many people wait so long on their back cast that their line has completely straightened out behind them. When the line straightens out completely in this manner, all the energy exerted backwards on the cast has been expended, the force of gravity is pulling the line down, and you're beginning to get an inactive or dead line. Instead, what you want to do is look back at your line, and when you see that it is beginning to take on the appearance of a "J", or a candy cane laid on its side, start sweeping your rod forward. This will help you load the rod properly for a good forward cast.

A FEW FINAL WORDS.

Remember that a back cast and a forward cast are executed in the just same way. What works to make a good back cast will work to make a good forward cast.

And keep in mind that the foundation of any cast is the back cast. I believe that 80 percent of the cast is the back cast. Make a good back cast and you can do a lot of things wrong on the forward cast and still be pretty effective. Despite that fact, most people won't take the trouble to turn around and look at their back cast. And after observing a lot of these casts, *I don't blame them!*

Anytime you are having trouble with your forward cast, turn around and take a look at what's happening behind you on the back cast. You'll probably discover the reason — or a least find a major contributing factor — for a poor forward cast.

Thank you for reading my little book. And good luck with your fly casting and fly fishing.

ABOUT LEFTY

The Editor-in-Chief and Principal Writer of *Lefty's Little Library of Fly Fishing* is Bernard "Lefty" Kreh. A member of the Fishing Hall of Fame, Lefty has been an active outdoor writer and photographer for almost four decades.

Until his retirement in 1990, Lefty was Outdoor Editor of *The Baltimore Sun*. Over the years he has held editorial staff positions with a number of prominent American fishing publications: most recently as Techniques Columnist for *Fishing World*, Fly Fishing Columnist for *Florida Sportsman*, Chief Editorial Advisor for *Flyfisher*, Editor-at-Large for *California Angler*, Fly Fishing Columnist for *Saltwater Sportsman*, and Editor-at-Large for *Fly Fisherman* magazines. In addition, he regularly provides feature articles to many other American and international fly fishing journals.

He is the author of a number of best-selling books on fly fishing and related activities, including *Salt Water Fly Patterns, L.L. Bean's Guide to Outdoor Photography, Advanced Fly Fishing Techniques, Fly Casting with Lefty Kreh, Spinning Tips, Salt Water Fly Fishing, Longer Fly Casting,* and with co-author Mark Sosin, *Fishing the Flats,* and *Practical Fishing Knots*.

He has been the featured performer in a number of videos, including *Fly Fishing New Zealand, Lefty Kreh's All New Fly Casting Techniques, Fishing the Bow River,* and *Lefty Kreh's Light Tackle Techniques*.

In addition to his numerous writings, Lefty has achieved equal fame as an outdoor photographer. He has served as photo consultant to L.L. Bean, for which organization he produced an outdoor photography video in 1987 which won Blue Ribbon Awards from the 1987 American Film and Video Festival and the Outdoor Writers of America.

Lefty has fly fished extensively in all 50 states, as well as the Bahamas, the Caribbean basin, Central and South America, Europe, the Pacific basin, Australia and New Zealand. At one time or another he has held 12 world's records for saltwater fish caught on a fly.

He frequently makes personal appearances at the major fly fishing conclaves through the United States, and is a most sought after speaker for annual meetings of fly fishing clubs in this country and abroad.

Because of his extensive writings, outdoor photography, and public speaking appearances in a distinguished career spanning almost four decades, Lefty Kreh may possibly be the most prominent — and is unquestionably the most popular — fly fishing professional in the world today.

INDEX